GERMAN BUSINESS CORRESPONDENCE

In the same series

French Business Correspondence
Stuart Williams and Nathalie McAndrew-Cazorla

Italian Business Correspondence
Vincent Edwards and Gianfranca Gessa Shepheard

Spanish Business Correspondence
Michael Gorman and María-Luisa Henson

French Business Situations*
Stuart Williams and Nathalie McAndrew-Cazorla

German Business Situations*
Paul Hartley and Gertrud Robins

Italian Business Situations*
Vincent Edwards and Gianfranca Gessa Shepheard

Spanish Business Situations*
Michael Gorman and María-Luisa Henson

Manual of Business French
Stuart Williams and Nathalie McAndrew-Cazorla

Manual of Business German
Paul Hartley and Gertrud Robins

Manual of Business Italian
Vincent Edwards and Gianfranca Gessa Shepheard

Manual of Business Spanish
Michael Gorman and María-Luisa Henson

*Accompanying cassettes available

GERMAN BUSINESS CORRESPONDENCE

Paul Hartley
and
Gertrud Robins

London and New York

Paul Hartley is Dean of the School of International Studies and Law at Coventry University.

Gertrud Robins is Lecturer in German at the East Warwickshire College, Rugby.

In the preparation of this handbook every effort was made to avoid the use of actual company names or trade names. If any has been used inadvertently, the publishers will change it in any future reprint if they are notified.

First published 1996
by Routledge
11 New Fetter Lane, London EC4P 4EE

Simultaneously published in the USA and Canada
by Routledge
29 West 35th Street, New York, NY 10001

© 1996 Paul Hartley and Gertrud Robins

Typeset in Rockwell and Univers by Solidus (Bristol) Ltd
Printed and bound in Great Britain by TJ Press (Padstow) Ltd, Cornwall

British Library Cataloguing in Publication Data
A catalogue record for this book is available from the British Library

Library of Congress Cataloguing in Publication Data
Hartley, Paul.
  German business correspondence/Paul Hartley and Gertrud Robins.
    p.   cm. – (Languages for business)
  English and German.
  1. Commercial correspondence, German.   I. Robins, Gertrud.
  II. Title.   III. Series.
HF5728.G3H34   1996
808'.066651031–dc20   96–19927
ISBN 0–415–13714–4

Contents

Business Correspondence

German commercial correspondence – some general notes

1 Note on translations

The documents presented here in parallel text are not a word-for-word translation of each other. Owing to obvious differences in letter-writing style in Germany, and the business terms used, it is possible to offer only an equivalent version of the German letter in the English text.

2 Letterheads

Various terms crop up consistently on German letterheads:

Betreff (sometimes *betrifft*): 're', 'subject'
Ihr Zeichen: your reference
Unser Zeichen: our reference
Ihre Nachricht vom: your letter of . . .

3 Opening sentences

The most usual opening sentences are now:

Sehr geehrte Herren (despite political correctness, still very widely used); *Sehr geehrte Damen und Herren*.

The singular form *Sehr geehrter Herr/Sehr geehrte Frau* is never used. *Frau* or *Herr* must be followed by the name or the designation of the addressee, for example:

Sehr geehrter Herr Oberstudiendirektor
Sehr geehrte Frau Oberstudienrätin
Sehr geehrter Herr Bulowski
Sehr geehrte Frau Schiller.

It was once very common to insert an exclamation mark after the opening: *Sehr geehrte Herren!*; *Sehr geehrte Frau Liesing!* This is now fast disappearing in favour of a comma:

Sehr geehrte Herren,

wir bestätigen den Empfang . . .

(note the use of the lower case letter after the comma.) OR in favour of open punctuation:

Sehr geehrte Frau Derrig

Wir haben soeben . . .

(in this case the first word of the letter begins with a capital letter).

4 Close of the letter

The most common formulation is *Mit freundlichen Grüßen*.

A very formal close, which is still used quite frequently but is losing popularity, is *Hochachtungsvoll*. Other possibilities are *Mit besten Grüßen* or *Mit bestem Gruß*.

5 Style

It is also important to note that, as in the case of English, the tendency now is to a more informal approach in letter writing, and toward the avoidance of excessive verbiage.

1 Enquiry about a product

Augustin SA
Z.I. de l'Empereur
F-19200 Ussel
France

Dear Sir/Madam

RE: TOOTHPICK MAKING & PACKAGING MACHINE

We represent a major distributor of foodstuffs and related materials.

We have found your name in *Kompass* under the category of suppliers of toothpick-making machinery. Our present requirement is for a special toothpick-making and packaging machine. If you do produce such equipment or can supply it we would be pleased to receive your earliest quotation CIF Mombasa, prices for this machine and its equipment, together with a stated delivery time.

Please would you also quote for the installation of this machine in the Ususu factory in Mombasa.

We look forward to your earliest reply and remain

Yours faithfully

John Mason
Technical Director

1 Produktanfrage

Storsberg Maschinen GmbH
Franzensstr. 34

D–38441 Einbeck

<u>Gerät zur Herstellung und Verpackung von Zahnstochern</u>

Sehr geehrte Damen und Herren,[1]

wir vertreten ein Großhandelsunternehmen von Lebensmitteln und branchenverwandten Waren.

Wir fanden Ihren Namen in 'Kompass' klassifiziert als Lieferant von Geräten zur Zahnstocherherstellung. Zur Zeit benötigen wir eine Spezialmaschine für die Erzeugung und Verpackung von Zahnstochern. Wenn Sie derartige Geräte herstellen oder liefern, wären wir Ihnen dankbar für Ihr baldmöglichstes Angebot CIF Mombasa, Preise für diese Maschine samt Zubehör sowie Angabe der Lieferzeit.

Könnten Sie uns auch eine Preisangabe für die Installierung dieser Maschine in der Ususu Fabrik in Mombasa zukommen lassen.[2]

Wir freuen uns, so bald wie möglich von Ihnen zu hören und verbleiben[3]

mit besten Grüßen

Gianni Mussini
Technischer Leiter

1 *Sehr geehrte Damen und Herren*: this opening is gaining in popularity, but *Sehr geehrte Herren* is still quite common.
2 *Zukommen lassen*: this is very formal, but in common use. *Schicken* or *senden* would also be possible.
3 *Und verbleiben*: the use of this phrase is not strictly necessary.

2 Enquiry about prices

Bandani Detergenti SpA
Via A. Lamarmora 75
20093 COLOGNO MONZESE (MI)
Italy

Dear Sir/Madam

RE: QUOTATION RMS34/16 JAN 199-/TOILET CLEANSER

On 16 January we received a quotation from your company for the supply of 4,000 litres of industrial toilet cleanser and disinfectant. We were unable to justify ordering this at the time, because we had sufficient stocks from our previous order at the end of last year.

We would like to enquire now if the prices quoted at the time are still valid for this commodity.

If you are unequivocably able to confirm that this is the case, please take this letter as an order for a further 10,000 litres. If there has been any price increase, please fax this to us or phone the undersigned to enable us to proceed and agree a price in due course.

Yours faithfully

Dick DeZwart
Buyer

2 Preisanfrage

Fa Volker & Roth[1]
Grabenzeile 14

D 04251 Leipzig

Betreff: Preisangabe RMS34/16.01.9-/Toilettenreiniger

Sehr geehrte Damen und Herren,

am 16.01. erhielten wir eine Preisangabe von Ihrer Firma bezüglich der Lieferung von 4000l Toilettenreinigungs- und Desinfektionsmittel[2] für Industriezwecke. Da wir noch genügend Vorrat von unserer vorherigen Bestellung am Ende letzten Jahres hatten, fanden wir einen Auftrag zu dieser Zeit nicht gerechtfertigt.

Nun möchten wir gerne anfragen, ob die damals angegebenen Preise für diese Ware noch gültig sind.

Wenn Sie eindeutig bestätigen können, daß dies der Fall ist, dann betrachten Sie bitte dieses Schreiben als Auftrag für weitere 10 000l. Im Falle[3] einer Preissteigerung faxen Sie uns bitte oder rufen Sie mich an, sodaß wir zu gegebener Zeit zu einer Preisabsprache kommen können.

Mit besten Grüßen

F. DeZwart
Einkäufer

1 *Fa*: abbreviation of 'Firma'.
2 *Toilettenreinigungs-*: note that the second part of the compound noun is contained in the following noun (*Desinfektionsmittel*).
3 *Im Falle einer Preissteigerung*: avoids a verbal construction (*wenn wir . . .*). Note that *Preiserhöhung* would be a suitable alternative.

3 Enquiry about a company

Giardin Prati SpA
Via Cassia Km 89
Val di Paglia
53040 RADICOFANI
Siena
Italy

Dear Sir/Madam

RE: ORDER LAWN-IND/CZ28

We refer to your quotation for 30 industrial mowing machines, model CZ28.

Our client is now eager to proceed with finalizing the order for this equipment as we are slowly approaching spring time. As we have never placed an order with your company, we would like to receive your full audited accounts for the last four trading years.

Please ensure that the above accounts reach us within the next five working days, as we are eager not to miss the six-week delivery time which will enable us to have the equipment in our hands as soon as possible.

Yours faithfully

Sales Department

3 Firmenanfrage

Gartenwies GmbH[1]
Lilienstr. 15

A 6020 Innsbruck

Betr.: Auftrag MÄH-IND/CZ28

Sehr geehrte Damen und Herren,

wir beziehen uns auf Ihre Preisangabe für Großmähmaschinen, Typ CZ28.

Wegen des bevorstehenden Frühjahrsbeginns möchte unser Kunde unbedingt den Auftrag für diese Geräte abschließen. Da wir aber Ihrer Firma noch nie einen Auftrag erteilt haben,[2] wären wir dankbar, Ihre Bücher der letzten vier Geschäftsjahre geprüft zu erhalten.

Bitte veranlassen Sie, daß uns die obigen Bücher bestimmt innerhalb der nächsten fünf Arbeitstage erreichen, da wir die sechswöchige Lieferfrist keineswegs versäumen möchten, um die Geräte baldmöglichst[3] zur Hand zu haben.

Hochachtungsvoll

Luigi Ravanelli
Verkaufsabteilung

1 GmbH: *Gesellschaft mit beschränkter Haftung* (company with limited liability).
2 *Einen Auftrag erteilen*: 'place an order'. *Einen Auftrag geben* would also be possible.
3 *Baldmöglichst*: very common in commercial correspondence. *So bald wie möglich* also possible.

4 Enquiry about a person

ROPER Industriale
Viale San Benedetto 39–43
20084 Lacchiarella
Milano

Dear Sirs

RE: Mr Samuel Smith

We write to you as a fellow producer of machine tools. We have recently received an application from Mr Samuel Smith of Reading (England). He is applying for a post as technical support engineer with our company and has given your company's name both as a previous employer and as a character referee.

From our reading of Mr Smith's CV he would appear most suitable for the post. However, we are also keen that people should fit into our factory and we are most concerned that in his early twenties Mr Smith was a very active member of the European Pro-Whale Organization. We would appreciate your comments on this as we are keen to be better informed about this candidate.

Yours faithfully

Carlo Ruggeri
Personnel Manager

4 Einholung einer Personalreferenz

EFI Maschinenbau
Postfach 2340

D–70414 Stuttgart

Betrifft: Referenz für Herrn Günther Schmidt[1]

Sehr geehrte Damen und Herren,

Wir möchten uns an Sie als Kollegen in der Werkzeugmaschinenbranche in folgender Angelegenheit wenden:

Vor kurzem erhielten wir eine Bewerbung von Herrn Günther Schmidt aus Passau. Er sucht bei uns um die Stelle als Hilfstechniker an und gab Ihre Firma als früheren Arbeitgeber und als Charakterreferenz an.

Seinem Lebenslauf nach zu beurteilen erscheint uns Herr Schmidt als äußerst fähig.

Da wir jedoch großen Wert auf Anpassungsfähigkeit in unserem Betrieb legen und uns Herrn Schmidts aktive Mitgliedschaft bei der Europa-Organisation 'Rettet den Wal' in seinen Zwanzigern[2] etwas zu denken gibt, wären wir über Ihren Kommentar zu unserer besseren Information über den Bewerber äußerst dankbar.

Mit besten Grüßen

Carlo Ruggeri
Firmeninhaber

1 *Betrifft*: note the use of the verb as an alternative to *Betreff*.
2 *In seinen Zwanzigern*: 'in his twenties'. Note however: 'in the twenties' (period) is *in den zwanziger Jahren*.

5 Enquiry asking for a specific quote

Sales Manager
OFFICE 2000
89–91 Scott Road
Olton
Solihull
West Midlands
B92 7RZ

Dear Sir/Madam

RE: LASER PHOTOCOPIER PR3000

We have been in correspondence with your company over the last six months and have in that time received a number of different quotations for different models of the industrial laser photocopying machines produced by your company. We have decided that the most suitable machine for our requirement is the PR3000.

We note however that your price of £4,000 was for one machine only. We are keen to purchase 20 printers of this particular model and we would like to know what your discount is on an order of this magnitude.

We are also keen to have the delivery time for this equipment. If it were possible to deliver the printers in two separate batches of 10 each, we would require the first delivery in three months' time and the second some two months after that, when our new British office is set up in Cromer.

Yours faithfully

Luca Evangelista
Sales Manager

5 Anfrage – Ersuchen um Spezialpreisangabe

Büro 2000
z. H. Verkaufsabteilung
Schottenstr. 89 91

D–27124 Bremen

Betr.: Laserphotokopiergerät PR 3000

Sehr geehrte Damen und Herren,

während unserer sechsmonatigen Geschäftsbeziehungen erhielten wir von Ihnen eine Reihe von Preisangaben für verschiedene Typen der von Ihnen hergestellten[1] Lasergroßkopiermaschinen.

Wir haben nun beschlossen, daß das für unsere Anforderungen am besten geeignete Gerät der Typ PR3000 ist.

Wir sehen aber, daß Ihr Preis von 9200 DM nur auf ein Gerät bezogen ist. Da wir jedoch 20 Kopierer dieses bestimmten Typs anschaffen[2] möchten, würden wir gerne Ihren Rabatt für einen Auftrag dieser Größenordnung erhalten.

Die Lieferfrist für die Geräte ist auch sehr wichtig für uns. Sollte es möglich sein, die Kopierer in zwei Teillieferungen von je 10 Stück zu senden, würden wir die erste Lieferung in drei Monaten und die zweite Lieferung in etwa zwei Monaten darauf benötigen, wenn unser neues Büro in München fertiggestellt ist.

Mit freundlichen Grüßen

G. Platini

1 This construction avoids a further clause (*der . . . Maschinen, die Sie hergestellt haben*).
2 *Anschaffen. Kaufen* would obviously also be possible.

6 Soliciting an agency

Erwin Page plc
Electrical appliances & supplies
29 Landon Place
London
SE45 9AS

Dear Sirs

We have heard from business associates that you are looking for an agency for the promotion of your products in the US and we feel that we may be of assistance to you.

We are a long established agency with offices in the midwest and on the west coast, and are experienced in the sale and promotion of domestic electrical equipment. We have helped several British firms to boost their US sales, and are convinced that you too could benefit from our experience. Our UK representative, Charles J Parker, would be pleased to call on you to discuss your needs further: you can contact him on 0171 745 4756. He will in any event be in your locality in the coming week, and will take the opportunity of calling on you.

Yours faithfully

Peter Bowles

6 Vertretungen – erste Kontaktnahme

Erwin Plattner GmbH
Industrieweg 27–29

D 61253 Frankfurt a. Main

Sehr geehrte Herren![1]

Von Geschäftsfreunden erfahren wir, daß Sie auf Suche nach einer Vertretung zur Einführung Ihrer Produkte in den Vereinigten Staaten sind, und wir glauben, daß wir Ihnen dabei behilflich sein könnten.

Wir sind eine gut eingeführte Agentur mit Büros im Mittelwesten und an der Westküste und haben Erfahrung im Verkauf und in der Verkaufsförderung von Elektrogeräten für den Haushalt.

Wir haben verschiedenen deutschen Firmen zu einer Absatzsteigerung in den USA verholfen und sind überzeugt, daß auch Sie von unserer Erfahrung profitieren würden.

Herr Friedrich Gärtner, unser Vertreter in Deutschland, wäre gerne bereit, Sie zu einer Besprechung Ihrer Bedürfnisse aufzusuchen.

Sie erreichen ihn unter[2] der Telefonnummer 071-23572. Er würde kommende Woche in Ihrer Gegend sein und könnte bei dieser Gelegenheit bei Ihnen vorsprechen.

Mit freundlichen Grüßen

Peter Bowles

1   *Sehr geehrte Herren!* The use of the exclamation mark in the opening is declining, but it is still occasionally found.
2   Note use of *unter*: on/at the following number.

7   Requesting information about agents

Duperrier SA
24 avenue des Sylphides
Brignoles
83170 Var
France

Dear Sirs

RE: LÜTTICH GmbH

We have heard from colleagues that you have recently used the services of
Lüttich GmbH as agents for your products in Germany. We are in a different line
of business from yourselves, but I believe that Lüttich represents companies of
various kinds. We are looking for agents in Germany and Switzerland for our
stationery products. I should be grateful if you could let us have further
information on the above-named firm. Any information you send us will be
treated with the strictest confidence.

Yours faithfully

P Brandauer

7 Erkundigung über Vertretung

Lettich GmbH
Postfach 4816

D–61422 Rüsselsheim

Sehr geehrte Damen und Herren,

wir hören von Geschäftskollegen,[1] daß Sie seit einiger Zeit die Dienste der Firma Duperrier SA als Vertretung Ihrer Waren in Frankreich in Anspruch nehmen.

Unsere Firmen sind zwar nicht branchenverwandt, aber wir glauben, daß Duperrier Unternehmen verschiedener Art vertritt.

Da wir Vetretungen für unsere Schreibwaren in Frankreich und in der Schweiz[2] suchen, wären wir Ihnen dankbar, wenn Sie uns weitere Informationen über die obige Firma könnten zukommen lassen.[3]

Wir werden Ihre Äußerungen selbstverständlich streng vertraulich behandeln.

Hochachtungsvoll

E. H. Porter

1 *Geschäftskollegen. Geschäftsfreunden* would also be possible.
2 Note *in der Schweiz*, as *Schweiz* is feminine. Also *in der Türkei*, etc.
3 Note the word order here. The finite verb precedes the two infinitives.

8 Giving information about agents

Herrn H Pike
Heinrich Pittmann GmbH
Ofterdingenstraße 69
D 68212 Mannheim
Germany

Dear Mr Pike

RE: DIETER & HELLER

Thank you for your enquiry about the company Dieter and Heller, who have been agents for our products for several years. This company has represented our interests in Eastern and Central Europe very effectively and our sales in those regions have been buoyant as a result. You will find their Bonn-based manager, Max Lettmann, particularly helpful, and I am sure he will be interested in co-operating with you.

If you do contact him, don't hesitate to mention my name.

Yours sincerely

Maria Fischer

8 Agenturauskunft

Herrn H. Pike
Heinrich Pittmann GmbH
Ofterdingenstr. 69

D–68212 Mannheim

Sehr geehrter Herr Pike,

wir danken Ihnen für Ihre Anfrage bezüglich der Firma Dieter und Heller, die seit Jahren die Vertretung unserer Waren innehat.

Ihre wirksame Vertretung unserer Interessen in Ost- und Mitteleuropa zog einen regen Absatz[1] unserer Produkte in diesen Gebieten nach sich.

Sie werden Herrn Max Lettmann, den Geschäftsleiter in Bonn, besonders entgegenkommend finden, und ich bin sicher, daß er an einer Zusammenarbeit mit Ihnen interessiert sein wird.

Wenn Sie sich mit ihm in Verbindung setzen, können Sie gerne meinen Namen erwähnen.

Mit freundlichen Grüßen

Maria Fischer

1 *Absatz* is invariably used in the singular, and usually preferred in correspondence to *Verkäufe*.

9 Request for a business reference

Mr G Le Blanc
Sales Director
CURTAINS & BLINDS Ltd
PO Box 181
Croydon
CR0 5SN

Dear Mr Le Blanc

RE: CASELLACCI SpA

We would like to introduce our company as a major supplier of castors for office furniture. We have been approached by Casellacci SPA of Pisa as potential distributors of our products in the Italian market. Mr Casellacci has explained that he has been supplying your range of curtain fittings in the Italian market for some fifteen years and has a proven track record of both successful sales and prompt payment with your company.

We are eager to proceed in the Italian market, but we wish to have some reassurance about this company, as we do not know either the company or the individuals concerned. It would appear that they are selling only high quality products and that our range of castors would fit very well into their sales range.

We would appreciate your earliest comments and thank you in advance for providing this information, which we would treat in the utmost confidence.

Yours sincerely

Steve Watwood
Export Manager

9 Ersuchen um Geschäftsreferenz

Fensterschön Gmbh
z.H. Herrn Georg Weiß, Verkaufsdirektor
Postfach 189
D 55314 Linz a. Rhein

Betr.: Casellacci SpA – Vertraulich[1]

Sehr geehrter Herr Weiß,

dürfen wir uns als Großlieferant von Möbelrollen für Büroeinrichtungen
vorstellen und in folgender Angelegenheit an Sie wenden:
Die Firma Casellacci SpA aus Pisa ist als möglicher Verteiler unserer Erzeugnisse
auf dem italienischen Markt an uns herangetreten.

Herr Casellacci erwähnte, daß er seit etwa 15 Jahren den italienischen Markt mit
Ihrem Vorhangzubehör beliefert. Er stellte auch seine Leistungen in bezug auf
Verkaufserfolg und Pünktlichkeit der Abrechnung mit Ihrer Firma unter Beweis.

Das Geschäft mit Italien liegt uns zwar sehr am Herzen, aber wir benötigen eine
gewisse Sicherheit, da uns weder die Firma noch Einzelpersonen der Firma
bekannt sind.

Es scheint, daß das Unternehmen nur erstklassige Waren verkauft und unser
Möbelrollensortiment ausgezeichnet in ihr Angebot[2] passen würde.

Wir würden uns freuen, so bald wie möglich von Ihnen zu hören und danken
Ihnen im voraus für Ihre Information, die wir streng vertraulich behandeln
werden.

Mit besten Grüßen

S. Watwood
Exportleiter

1 *Vertraulich*: 'confidential'. 'Strictly confidential' is *streng vertraulich*.
2 *Angebot*: 'offer' or (here) 'range'.

10 Favourable reply to request for a business reference

Mr S Watwood
CASTASSIST
158–161 Cressex Estate
New Malden
Surrey
KT13 4EY

Dear Mr Watwood

RE: CASELLACCI SpA of Pisa

We thank you for your letter of 11 March, regarding the company Casellacci of Italy as potential distributors of your range of castors.

We have indeed been working with Casellacci now for 23 years and know both Andrea Casellacci and his son Antonio, who has become more active in the company over the last few years. Casellacci have a number of most competent sales personnel covering the whole of Italy and the islands and have performed most effectively for our company against our large German competitors within the market. Casellacci have over this period of time proven to be most prompt in their payment. At the time of writing I cannot recall any undue delay in the settlement of their bills.

I have some awareness of your company and its products and I am sure they are suited to the Italian market. I hope the Casellacci company will prove a dependable and successful distributor for your product.

We hope you find this information sufficient to your requirements. Should you need any further comments please do not hesitate to contact us.

Yours sincerely

George Le Blanc
Sales Director

10 Günstige Geschäftsreferenz

Castassist
z.H. Herrn S. Watwood
158–161 Cressex Estate
New Malden
Surrey
KT13 4EY

Betrifft: Casellacci SpA, Pisa

Sehr geehrter Herr Watwood,

wir danken Ihnen für Ihren Brief vom 11.03. bezüglich der Firma Casellacci als potentieller Verteiler Ihrer Möbelrollen.

Es stimmt, daß wir seit 23 Jahren mit Casellacci zusammenarbeiten, und wir kennen sowohl Andrea Casellacci als auch seinen Sohn Antonio, der seit einigen Jahren in der Firma tätig ist.[1]

Casellacci beschäftigt tüchtige Verkaufskräfte, die für ganz Italien samt Inseln zuständig sind und für unsere Firma mit Erfolg gegenüber der französischen Konkurrenz[2] tätig waren.

Firma Casellacci zeigte sich immer pünktlich in ihren Zahlungen; ich weiß von keiner ungebührlichen Verzögerung in ihrer Abrechnung.

Mir ist Ihr Unternehmen teilweise bekannt, und ich bin sicher, daß Ihre Waren für den italienischen Markt geeignet sind. Ich hoffe, daß sich die Firma Casellacci als verläßlicher und erfolgreicher Verteiler Ihrer Produkte erweisen wird.

Wir hoffen, Ihnen mit dieser Auskunft gedient zu haben. Sollten Sie weitere Einzelheiten benötigen, bitte zögern Sie nicht, sich mit uns in Verbindung zu setzen.

Mit freundlichen Grüßen

Georg Weiß
Verkaufsleiter

1 Alternatives to *tätig ist*: *arbeitet*, or *beschäftigt ist*.
2 *Konkurrenz* can mean 'competition' or 'competitors'. 'Competitors' (lit.): *Konkurrenten*.

11 Unfavourable reply to request for a business reference

Mr S Watwood
CASTASSIST
158–161 Cressex Estate
New Malden
Surrey
KT13 4EY

Dear Mr Watwood

RE: CASELLACCI SpA OF PISA

We are in receipt of your letter regarding the company of Andrea Casellacci with whom you have been discussing the potential distribution of your products in the Italian market.

We must first ask you to accept our comments on this company in the most confidential terms. We have indeed been working with Casellacci for many years, but unfortunately six months ago Mr Andrea Casellacci was detained by the Italian police and certain irregularities within the company have come to light. A direct result of this situation, in our particular case, is that we have not received payment for the last three major shipments of goods to Casellacci, which were due to us at different times. We are at the moment in discussions with our solicitors who will be undertaking the appropriate action on our behalf.

It is our view, therefore, that although this company has performed successfully in the past, it is obviously not in a position to continue this work on our behalf and therefore it is fair to put to you that it would not be a suitable partner for you at this time.

Yours sincerely

George Le Blanc
Sales Director

11 Ungünstige Geschäftsreferenz

Castassist
z.H. Herrn S. Watwood
158–161 Cressex Estate New Malden
Surrey
KT13 4EY

Betr: Casellacci SpA, Pisa

Sehr geehrter Herr Watwood,

wir haben Ihren Brief bezüglich der Firma Casellacci erhalten, mit der Sie über den möglichen Vertrieb Ihrer Waren auf dem italienischen Markt im Gespräch sind.

Zunächst müssen wir Sie ersuchen, unsere Äußerungen über diese Firma mit strengster Vertraulichkeit zu behandeln. Wir haben zwar mit Casellacci längere Zeit zusammengearbeitet, aber Herr Andrea Casellacci war leider vor sechs Monaten in Polizeigewahrsam, und gewisse betriebliche Unregelmäßigkeiten stellten sich heraus.

Dieses Problem hatte zur Folge, daß wir unsererseits drei zu verschiedenen Terminen[1] fällige Zahlungen für Warenlieferungen an Casellacci noch nicht erhalten haben.

Zur Zeit besprechen wir die Angelegenheit mit unserem Anwalt, der in unserem Auftrag entsprechende Schritte unternehmen wird.

Aus unserer Sicht ist die Firma trotz guter Leistung in der Vergangenheit keineswegs mehr in der Lage, für uns weiter tätig zu sein, und daher ist es nur recht und billig, Ihnen offen zu sagen, daß die Firma Casellacci zur Zeit für eine Zusammenarbeit ungeeignet ist.

Mit besten Grüßen

Georg Weiß
Verkaufsleiter

1 *Termin* is a very common term in commercial correspondence, e.g. *ich habe einen Termin bei* ...: 'I have an appointment with ...'

12 Evasive reply to request for a business reference

Mr S Watwood
CASTASSIST
158–161 Cressex Estate
New Malden
Surrey
KT13 4EY

Dear Mr Watwood

RE: CASELLACCI SpA OF PISA/ITALY

We are in receipt of your letter regarding the company Casellacci SpA with whom you have been discussing the distribution of your products in the Italian market.

Casellacci are a very good company, but we are concerned that they might have already stretched themselves with the selling of our products in Italy. We feel that, if they did take on your range of products, they would probably have to employ a further product manager and perhaps another half a dozen regional sales people to cover the Italian market adequately.

We trust this information is sufficient, but should you require any further comments please do not hesitate to contact us.

Yours sincerely

George Le Blanc
Sales Director

12 Ausweichende Antwort auf Ersuchen um Geschäftsreferenz

Castassist
z.H. Herrn S. Watwood
158–161 Cressex Estate
New Malden
Surrey
KT13 4EY

Betr: Casellacci SpA, Pisa

Sehr geehrter Herr Watwood,

wir haben Ihr Schreiben bezüglich der Firma Casellacci erhalten, mit der Sie über den Verkauf Ihrer Waren auf dem italienischen Markt in Verhandlung stehen.[1]

Casellacci ist ein sehr guter Betrieb, aber wir fürchten, daß er mit dem Vertrieb unserer Waren in Italien bereits voll ausgelastet ist.

Bei Übernahme Ihres Sortiments, glauben wir, würde wahrscheinlich der Einsatz eines weiteren Produktleiters und weiterer sechs Gebietsvertreter zur ausreichenden Erfassung[2] des italienischen Marktes notwendig sein.

Wir hoffen, daß diese Information ausreichend ist. Sollten Sie jedoch weitere Einzelheiten benötigen, bitte zögern Sie nicht, sich mit uns in Verbindung zu setzen.

Mit freundlichen Grüßen

Georg Weiß
Verkaufsleiter

1 *In Verhandlung stehen*: 'be in negotiations with'.
2 *Zur* plus the noun avoids a long verbal construction (*um ... zu*, or *damit wir ... können*).

13   Placing an order

Jenkins Freeman plc
Unit 36
Heddington Industrial Estate
Birmingham
B34 9HF

Dear Sirs

We thank you for your catalogue and price list, which we read with interest. On the basis of your current prices, we wish to order the following:

    50 electric drills, model 1456/CB
    50 chain saws, model 1865/CH

Delivery is required by 3.5.199-, and the goods should be delivered to our warehouse in Riddington Way, Battersea. As agreed, payment will be by banker's draft.

Yours faithfully

Gillian Brookes
Purchasing Department

13 Auftragserteilung

Jeschke und Freimann GmbH
Industriepark Süd
Standplatz 12

D–40697 Düsseldorf

Sehr geehrte Herren,

wir danken Ihnen für Ihren Katalog samt[1] Preisliste, die wir mit Interesse zur Kenntnis genommen haben.

Auf der Basis Ihrer derzeitigen Preise möchten wir Ihnen folgenden Auftrag erteilen:

50 Elektrobohrer, Typ 1456/CB
50 Kettensägen, Typ 1865/CH

Die Lieferung wird bis 03.05. benötigt,[2] mit Zustellung der Waren an unser Lagerhaus in Riddington Way, Battersea. Zahlung durch Wechsel, wie vereinbart.[3]

Mit besten Grüßen

Gillian Brookes
Einkauf

1 *Samt* is very formal, and would rarely, if ever, be used in spoken German.
2 *Bis*: 'up to and including'. Strictly speaking, 'before' would be *vor*.
3 Note the contracted form of this sentence. There is a tendency towards this style in commercial correspondence.

14 Cancellation of order

Porzellanfabrik Hering
Langauer Allee 18
D–70102 Stuttgart
Germany

Dear Sirs

RE: ORDER NO. HGF/756

We recently placed an order for 60 bone china coffee sets (model 'Arcadia'). The order reference: HGF/756.

We regret that due to circumstances beyond our control, we now have to cancel the order. We apologize for any inconvenience this may cause you.

Yours faithfully

D Grey

14 Widerrufung einer Bestellung

Porzellanfabrik Hering
Langauer Allee 18

D 70102 Stuttgart

Sehr geehrte Damen und Herren,

wir stellten Ihnen neulich einen Auftrag über[1] 60 Porzellan Kaffeeservices (Typ 'Arcadia') unter Bestellnummer HGF/756.

Umständehalber müssen wir diesen Auftrag leider widerrufen, und wir bitten für alle dadurch entstandenen Unannehmlichkeiten vielmals um Entschuldigung.

Mit freundlichen Grüßen

D. Grey

1 *Auftrag über*: 'order for'. *Erteilen* could also be used instead of *stellen*.

15 Confirming a telephone order

Henning & Söhne GmbH
Schillerstraße 45
D–43002 Essen
Germany

Dear Mr Hartmann

Following the visit of your representative Dieter Höne last week, we are confirming our telephone order for

    250 car seat covers, model AS/385/C

The total price of the order, inclusive of your discount, is £4,600. Payment will follow immediately upon delivery. The covers should be delivered by Tuesday 3 February, to our warehouse on the Pennington Industrial Estate, Rochdale.

Yours sincerely

Derek Batty

15 Bestätigung eines telephonischen Auftrags

Henning & Söhne GmbH
Schillerstraße 45

D 43002 Essen

Sehr geehrter Herr Hartmann,

im Anschluß an den Besuch Ihres Vertreters Herrn Dieter Höne in der letzten
Woche bestätigen wir unseren telephonischen Auftrag über

   250 Autositzüberzüge, Typ AS/385/C

Der Gesamtpreis für die Bestellung beträgt 4600 Pfund,[1] inklusive[2] Rabatt.
Zahlung unmittelbar nach Erhalt[3] der Lieferung.

Die Überzüge sollten bis Dienstag, 3. Februar an unser Lagerhaus,
Industriegelände Pennington, Rochdale, geliefert werden.

Mit besten Grüßen

Derek Batty

1 *Pfund*: note the use of the singular. (50 *Mark*: 50 Marks).
2 Alternative to *inklusive*: *einschließlich*.
3 *Unmittelbar nach Erhalt*: it is common to omit the definite article in such expressions in
   commercial correspondence.

16 Making an order for specific items of office equipment

Your ref.
Our ref. HB/LP

Garzón y Hijos
Plaza de la Catedral 8
Bogotá

Dear Sir/Madam

Please supply the following items, using the Order Number E183, to the above address at your earliest convenience; payment will be made within 14 days of receipt of your invoice and of the goods as ordered.

  6 artists' stools (aluminium)

  20 sets of 5 painting brushes

  10 reams of A5 drawing paper

  2 drawing tables: 2m × 1m

  1 Sanchix camera: FB4X model

  1 QRM computer: portable TGs model

Before you prepare and invoice us for these goods, please inform us by telex or phone of the cost per item, in order to avoid any unexpectedly high sums in the final bill, as this is something which has occasionally happened in the past.

We thank you in anticipation of your prompt reply.

Yours faithfully

Herberto Baza
Studio Supervisor

16 Auftrag für spezielle Büroartikel

Firma Böcklin & Schiele
Ritterplatz 42b

50992 Leverkusen

Sehr geehrte Damen und Herren,

bitte senden Sie so bald wie möglich folgende Artikel an die obige Adresse unter Benutzung der Bestellnummer E183. Zahlung erfolgt innerhalb von zwei Wochen nach Erhalt der Rechnung und der bestellten Waren.

6 Malerschemel (Aluminium)
20 Garnituren zu je 5 Malerpinseln[1]
10 Ries A5 Zeichenpapier
2 Zeichentische 2m × 1m
1 Sanchix Photoapparat, Modell FB4X
1 QRM Computer, Modell TGs, tragbar

Bevor Sie uns diese Waren in Rechnung stellen, wären wir Ihnen dankbar, wenn Sie uns telefonisch oder per Fernschreiben[2] den Einzelpreis der Waren angeben könnten, da wir in der Vergangenheit manchmal unerwartet hohe Rechnungen erhalten haben.

Wir danken Ihnen im voraus für eine umgehende Antwort und verbleiben

mit besten Grüßen

Herbert Bart
Verwaltung

1 *Je*: 'each'. cf: *drei Bücher zu je 17 Mark*: 'three books at 17 Marks each'.
2 *Per Fernschreiben*: 'by telex'; by fax: *per Fax*.

17 Acknowledgement of an order

Mr Henry Putton
33 Flintway
West Ewell
Surrey
KT19 9ST

Dear Mr Putton

Thank you for your signed order given to our Adviser for a bed to be constructed to your specific requirements.

We shall now pass your order to our Design Department complete with your personal specification.

Delivery time will be in approximately seven weeks and you will be advised of the exact date in due course.

Once again many thanks for your order.

Yours sincerely

Janet Craig
Customer Relations Manager

17 Auftragsbestätigung

Herrn
Heinrich Pitter
Flintweg 33

D 04 Leipzig

Sehr geehrter Herr Pitter,

wir danken Ihnen für Ihre unserem Berater unterzeichnet übergebene Bestellung über ein für Ihre Bedürfnisse speziell angefertigtes Bett.[1]

Wir werden Ihren Auftrag samt Ihren Anweisungen an unsere Konstruktionsabteilung weiterleiten.

Die Lieferfrist beträgt etwa sieben Wochen und wir werden Ihnen das genaue Datum rechtzeitig bekanntgeben.

Nochmals besten Dank für Ihren Auftrag.[2]

Mit freundlichen Grüßen

Janet Craig
Kundendienst

1 The first paragraph has a very complex but compact structure. It avoids the use of several clauses, but care must be taken with the adjective endings.
2 Note the accusative. *Dank* is the object of the understood verb.

18 Payment of invoices – letter accompanying payment

Dr V Meyer
Neue Marktforschung GmbH
Kastanienallee 14
D–45023 Osnabrück
Germany

Dear Dr Meyer

I enclose an international money order to the value of 450DM as payment for the three market research reports published by your organization this year.

As agreed during our telephone conversation on 15.1.199-, the sum enclosed includes postage.

I look forward to receiving the reports as soon as possible.

Yours sincerely

Maria Meller

Enc.

18 Begleitbrief zur Begleichung einer Rechnung

Frau
Dr. V. Meyer
Neue Marktforschung GmbH
Kastanienallee 14

D 45023 Osnabrück

Sehr geehrte Frau Dr. Meyer,

in der Anlage[1] finden Sie eine internationale Postanweisung im Werte von DM 4500 als Zahlung für drei von Ihrer Organisation in diesem Jahr veröffentlichte Marktberichte.

Wie am 15.01.199- telefonisch vereinbart, enthält dieser Betrag auch die Postgebühr.

Wir freuen uns darauf, die Berichte so bald wie möglich zu erhalten.

Mit besten Grüßen

Maria Weller

Anlage
Internationale Postanweisung

1 Alternatives to *in der Anlage: als Anlage, beiliegend, beigelegt,* or *wir legen ... bei.*

19 Payment of invoices – request for deferral

South East Finance Ltd
Dovehouse Lane
Sutton
Surrey
SM2 6LY

Dear Sirs

RE: MAXITRUCK 2000

I refer to our recent agreement of 30 November 199- regarding payment for one 40-ton Maxitruck 2000.

As you will recall, we paid an initial instalment of £10,000 and agreed to 10 further monthly instalments of £3,000. The December and January instalments, as you will know, have been paid promptly.

However, owing to the serious economic situation we find ourselves in, we are at the moment unable to make payments as agreed. Because of our reduced cash flow we are unable to pay more than £2,000 a month. We would, therefore, appreciate the opportunity to discuss this matter with you and reach a mutually satisfactory arrangement.

Yours faithfully

Tom Page
Finance Manager

19 Rechnungsbegleichung –
Bitte um Stundung

Süd-Ost Finanzen GmbH
Taubenschlagweg 12

D 44003 Dortmund

Sehr geehrte Damen und Herren,

wir beziehen uns auf unsere jüngste Absprache am 30.11.199- bezüglich der
Zahlung für den 40t Großlaster Maxi 2000.

Wie Sie sich erinnern werden, bezahlten wir eine anfängliche Rate von 23 000 DM
und vereinbarten weitere zehn Monatsraten zu je 6900 DM.[1] Die Raten für
Dezember und Januar wurden, wie Sie wissen, pünktlich überwiesen.[2]

Da wir uns zur Zeit jedoch in wirtschaftlichen Schwierigkeiten befinden, sind wir
leider nicht in der Lage, den Zahlungen, wie vereinbart, nachzukommen.

Aufgrund von begrenzter Liquidität können wir nicht mehr als 4600 DM pro
Monat aufbringen. Wir wären Ihnen daher dankbar für eine Gelegenheit, diesen
Punkt zur beiderseitigen Zufriedenstellung mit Ihnen erörtern zu können.

Mir freundlichen Grüßen

Tom Page
Finanzleiter

1 *Zu je 6900 Mark*: 'at 6900 Marks each'.
2 *Überweisen*: 'to transfer'. 'To transfer to an account': *auf ein Konto überweisen*.

20 Payment of invoices – refusal to pay

Johnson (Builders) Ltd
Nugget Grove
Christchurch

Dear Sirs

RE: INVOICE NO. L28/4659

We refer to your invoice No. L28/4659 regarding repairs to the roof of workshop 17 at Heath End.

In spite of the repair work carried out by your employees the roof still leaked in a number of places during the recent rains, causing a shut-down of the workshop for safety reasons.

We look forward to a speedy response by you to resolve this problem and assure you that your invoice will be paid as soon as this matter has been resolved to our satisfaction.

Yours faithfully

20 Zahlungsverweigerung

Baubetrieb Sieger
`Nußbaumstr. 2

27458 Bremen

Sehr geehrte Herren!

Wir beziehen uns auf Ihre Rechnung Nr. L28/4659 betreffend die Dachreparatur unserer Werkstatt 17 in der Heidenstraße.

Trotz der von Ihren Arbeitern durchgeführten Reparatur erwies sich das Dach während des neulichen Regens an mehreren Stellen als undicht, was eine Schließung der Werkstatt aus Sicherheitsgründen zur Folge hatte.

Wir erwarten nun, daß Sie unverzüglich Schritte zur Lösung dieses Problems unternehmen, und versichern Ihnen, daß Ihre Rechnung beglichen wird, sobald diese Angelegenheit zu unserer Zufriedenheit beigelegt ist.

Hochachtungsvoll[1]

M. Meier

1 Although *Hochachtungsvoll* is declining in popularity, it is still appropriate in letters of this type which are making a complaint/demanding payment, etc.

21 Apologies for non-payment

Mr I Sahani
Michigan Lake Trading Co.
974 South La Salle Street
Chicago
Illinois 60603
USA

Dear Mr Sahani

I refer to our telephone conversation yesterday.

I must once again apologize for the fact that you have not yet received payment for order No. 072230/5310.

Payment was duly authorized by me on the 10 July, but due to staff holidays the paperwork appears to have gone astray between our sales and finance departments.

We have now traced the relevant documentation and I can assure you that the matter is being attended to with the utmost urgency.

If you do not receive payment by Monday, 22 August, I would be grateful if you would contact me immediately.

I apologize once again for the inconvenience this has caused you and assure you of our best intentions.

Yours sincerely

21 Entschuldigung für Nichtbegleichung einer Rechnung

Firma Bergmann & Co
z.H. Herrn F. Sacher
Blücherweg 27

D–14800 Berlin

Sehr geehrter Herr Sacher,

darf ich mich noch einmal dafür entschuldigen, daß Sie noch keine Bezahlung für Auftrag Nr. 072230/5310 erhalten haben.

Zwar habe ich ordnungsgemäß die Zahlung am 10. Juli veranlaßt, doch die Unterlagen schienen wegen Personalurlaub in der Verkaufs- und der Rechnungsabteilung in Verlust geraten zu sein.

Wir haben aber nun die diesbezüglichen Papiere gefunden, und ich kann Ihnen versichern,[1] daß die Angelegenheit als äußerst dringlich behandelt wird.

Sollten Sie die Zahlung bis Montag, 22. August nicht erhalten haben, wäre ich Ihnen dankbar, wenn Sie sich mit mir sofort in Verbindung setzen könnten.

Ich entschuldige mich noch einmal für die Ihnen verursachten Unannehmlichkeiten und verspreche Ihnen, daß solche Irrtümer nicht wieder vorkommen werden.

Mit besten Grüßen

J. Yipp

1 Note the use of the dative after *versichern* in this sense. 'I assure you of my support': *Ich versichere Sie meiner Unterstützung* (accusative + genitive).

22 Request for payment

Huron Motor Factors
6732 John Street
Markham
Ontario
Canada L3R 1B4

Dear Sir

RE: INVOICE NO. JE/17193

As per our invoice JE/17193 of 13.3.199-, we supplied your Nashlee plant with 500 litres of AVC automotive base paint, payment due 60 days after receipt of our consignment.

This period of time has now elapsed and we request immediate settlement of the above invoice.

Yours faithfully

22 Zahlungsaufforderung

XY Motorwerke
Rennweg 27–29

21864 Hamburg

Sehr geehrte Herren,

gemäß unserer Rechnung JE/17193 vom 13.03.9- belieferten wir Ihr Kieler Werk mit 500l AVC Fahrzeuggrundierlack, Zahlung 60 Tage nach Erhalt der Lieferung.

Diese Frist ist nun abgelaufen und wir erwarten die sofortige Begleichung der obigen Rechnung.

Hochachtungsvoll[1]

J. Renner

1 *Hochachtungsvoll* is preferred in view of the overall tone of the letter.

23 Overdue account

First letter

Lota (UK) Ltd
93 Armstrong Road
Dudley
West Midlands DY3 6EJ

Dear Sir

Arrears on Finance Agreement No. 261079

I am writing to advise you that your bankers have failed to remit the April instalment of £8,373 on the above agreement and as a result the account is now in arrears.

This has incurred an additional £460.50 in interest and administration charges.

Please advise your bank to transfer £8,873 to our account to bring your account up to date and enable us to remove it from our arrears listing.

Yours faithfully

23 Überfällige Rechnung

Erste Mahnung

LOTA GmbH
Färberstr. 38

51357 Köln

Betr.: Zahlungsabkommem Nr. 261079 – Rückstände

Sehr geehrte Damen und Herren,

wir teilen Ihnen mit, daß Ihre Bank es verabsäumte, die Aprilrate von 19 257 DM bezügl. des obigen Abkommens zu überweisen, und daß Sie daher im Zahlungsrückstand sind.

Dazu kommen noch DM 1059,15 für Zinsen und Verwaltungsgebühren.

Bitte beauftragen Sie Ihre Bank, DM 19 257 auf unser Konto als Ausgleich zu überweisen,[1] sodaß Sie nicht mehr auf der Liste unserer Rückstände aufscheinen.

Mit vorzüglicher Hochachtung[2]

D. Bursche

1 *Auf unser Konto*: 'to our account'.
2 This expression is very formal, and would be avoided by many writers.

24 Overdue account

Final letter

Lota (UK) Ltd
93 Armstrong Road
Dudley
West Midlands DY3 6EJ

Dear Sir

Arrears on Finance Agreement No. 261079

Our records show that despite our previous reminders, your account remains overdue.

We must now insist that you clear the outstanding arrears by close of business on Friday, 26 June 199-.

Failure to comply with this request by the date specified will result in the termination of the agreement. We will then take steps to recover our property.

Yours faithfully

24 Überfällige Rechnung

Letzte Warnung

LOTA GmbH
Färberstr. 38

51357 Köln

Betreff: Zahlungsabkommen Nr. 261079 – Rückstände

Sehr geehrte Damen und Herren,

aus unseren Unterlagen geht hervor,[1] daß Ihre Rechnung trotz vorhergehender Mahnungen weiterhin überfällig ist.

Wir müssen nun darauf bestehen,[2] daß Sie Ihren Zahlungsrückstand bis Geschäftsschluß am 26. Juni 199- bereinigen.

Sollten Sie dieser Aufforderung bis zum angegebenen Datum nicht Folge leisten, wird dies die Kündigung Ihres Abkommens nach sich ziehen und wir werden Schritte zur Rückzahlung unserer Forderungen in die Wege leiten.

Hochachtungsvoll

D. Bursche

1 Also possible: *wir (er)sehen aus unseren Unterlagen* ...
2 When used with a noun, *bestehen auf* is used with the dative (*ich bestehe auf sofortiger Begleichung*).

25 Job advertisement

newspaper

H J Marketing Services
County House
53 Stukely Street
Twickenham TW1 7LA

Dear Sir

Please would you insert the attached job advertisement in the January issues of *East European Marketing Monthly* and *Food Industry Digest*.

As usual we require a quarter-page ad, set according to our house style.

Please invoice payment in the usual way.

Yours faithfully

Enc.

25 Stellenanzeige

Brief an Zeitung

MVS Marketing
Gärtnerweg 18

68523 Wiesbaden

Sehr geehrte Damen und Herren,

bitte setzen die beiliegende Stellenanzeige in die Januar-Ausgabe des
'Osteuropäischen Marktanzeigers' und des 'Informationsblattes für die
Lebensmittelindustrie'.

Wie gewöhnlich benötigen wir ein viertelseitiges Inserat im von unserer Firma
bevorzugten Layout.

Wir erbitten Rechnungsstellung wie üblich.[1]

Mit besten Grüßen

D. Herder

Anlage
Stellenanzeige

1 *Wir erbitten*: *wir bitten um* . . . would also be possible.

26 Newspaper advertisement

We are now expanding our operations in Eastern Europe and require experienced people within the food processing industry who are looking for an opportunity to sell in Hungary and Bulgaria products of leading food companies. The products are of good quality and already enjoy a substantial international reputation.

The salary for the above position is negotiable dependent upon experience and qualifications. A competitive benefits package is also offered.

For further details and application form please write to the Personnel Manager, EEF Ltd, Roman Road, Epsom, Surrey, KT72 7EF, quoting reference HB/127.

Closing date: 14 February 199-.

27 Asking for further details and application form

EEF Ltd
Roman Road
Epsom
Surrey KT72 7EF

Dear Sir

Ref. HB/127

I would be grateful if you could send me further details and an application form for the post of sales manager advertised in this month's *East European Marketing Monthly.*

Yours faithfully

26 Stellenanzeige

Zur Erweiterung unserer Geschäftstätigkeit in Osteuropa benötigen wir Mitarbeiter mit Erfahrung in der nahrungsmittelverarbeitenden Industrie für die Suche nach[1] Verkaufsmöglichkeiten von Produkten führender Lebensmittelfirmen in Ungarn und Bulgarien. Es handelt sich dabei um Spitzenprodukte[2] von erheblichem internationalem Ruf.

Gehalt für obige Stellung nach Vereinbarung, abhängig von Erfahrung und Qualifikation. Wir bieten auch ein zusätzliches Leistungspaket, das sich sehen lassen kann.

Für weitere Einzelheiten bzw.[3] Bewerbungsformulare schreiben Sie bitte an die Personalleitung, EEF GmbH, Römerstr.19, 67000 Mainz, unter Angabe von Zeichen HB/127.

Einsendeschluß: 14. Februar 199-

1 *Die Suche nach*: 'the search for'.
2 *Spitzenprodukte*: 'leading products'. cf. *Spitzenpolitiker*: 'leading politician'.
3 *Bzw.*, abbreviation for *beziehungsweise*: 'or'.

27 Bitte um weitere Einzelheiten und Bewerbungsformular

EEF GmbH
Personalabteilung
Römerstr.19

67000 Mainz

Zeichen: HB/127

Sehr geehrte Damen und Herren,

ich wäre Ihnen dankbar für die Übersendung von weiteren Einzelheiten sowie einem Bewerbungsformular für die Stellung als Verkaufsleiter, für die Sie im 'Osteuropäischen Marktanzeiger' dieses Monats inserieren.

Mit freundlichen Grüßen

28   Job application

25 January 199-

Black's (Automotive) Ltd
18 Dawson Street
Birmingham
B24 4SU

Dear Sir

I am applying for the post of market research officer advertised in the *Guardian* on 21.1.9-.

I graduated from Chiltern University in June with an upper second class degree in European Business. The following January I was awarded the Diploma of the Chartered Institute of Marketing. On my degree course I specialized in market research and did a one-year work placement with Cox, Paton and Taylor in London.

Since leaving university I have been employed as a market research assistant in the Quantocks Tourist Agency. I am now seeking an opportunity to apply the knowledge and skills I have acquired in a larger, more market-orientated organization.

I enclose a CV and the names of two referees. I would be grateful if you would not contact my current employer without prior reference to me.

Yours faithfully

Michael Westwood

Enc.

28 Bewerbungsschreiben

25. Januar 199-

Kfz Handel Schwarz
Valentinstr. 76

62345 München

Sehr geehrte Damen und Herren,

ich möchte mich um die Stellung als Mitarbeiter in der Marktforschung bewerben gemäß Ihrer Anzeige in der Süddeutschen Zeitung vom 21.01.9-.[1]

Im Juni schloß ich mein Studium der Europäischen Betriebswirtschaft an der Universität Bochum mit gutem Erfolg ab. Im folgenden Januar erwarb ich das Staatsdiplom in Marketing. Während meines Studiums wählte ich Marktforschung als Spezialfach[2] und machte in diesem Zusammenhang ein einjähriges Praktikum bei der Firma Cox, Paton & Taylor in London.

Seit dem Ende meines Studiums bin ich als Marktforschungsassistent beim Reiseunternehmen DEG tätig. Jetzt suche ich nach einer Gelegenheit, meine erworbenen Kenntnisse und Fähigkeiten in einer größeren, stärker marktorientierten Organisation anzuwenden.

Ich lege einen Lebenslauf sowie die Namen von zwei Referenzen bei und wäre dankbar für Ihre Mitteilung, wenn Sie meinen Arbeitgeber kontaktieren.

Mit besten Grüßen

Michael Oswald

Anlage
Lebenslauf

1 *Bewerben* could have been placed at the end of the sentence.
2 *Spezialfach*: 'specialist subject'. Note also *Hauptfach* ('main subject'); *Nebenfach* ('subsidiary subject').

29 Curriculum vitae

Surname:	Cording
First names:	Donald Maurice
Date of Birth:	18 March 1959

QUALIFICATIONS: BA (Hons) Business Studies (Leeds, 1981)
MBA (Warwick, 1985)

CURRENT EMPLOYMENT:
(Sept. 1988 to the present)   Marketing Manager, Cockpit Industries Ltd,
8 Wendover Road, Accrington, Lancs.
BB7 2RH

PREVIOUS EMPLOYMENT:
(a) Jan. 1986–Sept. 1988:   Marketing Assistant,
Spurlands Ltd, 71 Misbourne Road,
Northallerton, Yorks. DL5 7YL

(b) Oct. 1981–Dec. 1985:   Marketing Assistant,
Tutton Enterprises Ltd, Wye House,
Cores End, Wolverhampton WV6 8AE

(c) Sept. 1979–July 1980:   Sales Assistant,
J V Ansell & Co., Greenaway Avenue,
Leek, Staffs. ST15 4EH

29 Lebenslauf

Familienname:	Cording
Vornamen:	Donald Maurice
Geburtsdatum:	18.03.59

QUALIFIKATIONEN: BA (Hons) Betriebswirtschaftslehre
Universität Leeds, 1981
MBA, Universität Warwick, 1985

GEGENWÄRTIGE STELLUNG: Marketing Manager, Cockpit Industries Ltd, 8
(seit Sept. 1988) Wendover Road, Accrington Lancs. BB7 2RH

FRÜHERE STELLUNGEN:
(a) Jan. 1986–Sept. 1988: Marketing Assistent, Spurlands Ltd, 71
Misbourne Road, Northallerton, Yorks. DL5
7YL

(b) Okt. 1981–Dez. 1985: Marketing Assistent, Tutton Enterprizes Ltd,
Wye House, Cores End, Wolverhampton WV6
8AE

(c) Sept. 1979–Juli 1980: Verkäufer, J V Ansell & Co., Greenaway Ave,
Leek, Staffs. ST15 4EH

30 Unsolicited letter of application

Executive Agency plc
22 Ellison Place
London WC1B 1DP

Dear Sirs

I have recently returned to Britain after working in Canada and the Gulf States for the last 15 years.

I spent five years in Canada as chief financial accountant of Bourges-Canada in Montreal, before moving to the Gulf. I have worked there as financial director for Jenkins-Speller for the last ten years. During this period the company's number of clients and turnover have quadrupled.

I have returned to Britain for family reasons and I am now seeking an appropriate position in a company that can capitalize on my expertise in financial management and strategy.

I enclose a detailed CV for your further information and look forward to hearing from you soon.

Yours faithfully

R Bennett

Enc.

30 Stellenbewerbung ohne vorherige Anzeige

Stellenvermittlung GmbH
Elisenplatz 22

80000 München

Sehr geehrte Damen und Herren,

nach 15 Jahren beruflicher Tätigkeit in Kanada und in den Golfstaaten bin ich seit einiger Zeit wieder zurück in Deutschland.

Ich war fünf Jahre Hauptbuchhalter bei der Firma Bourges-Canada in Montreal und übernahm dann eine Stellung in den Golfstaaten, wo ich die letzten zehn Jahre als Finanzleiter der Firma Jenkins-Speller tätig war. Während dieser Zeit vergrößerten sich Umsatz- sowie Kundenzahlen um ein Vierfaches.[1]

Ich bin aus familiären Gründen nach Deutschland zurückgekehrt und suche nun eine geeignete Stellung bei einem Unternehmen, dem meine Sachkenntnis der Finanzleitung und -planung von Nutzen sein kann.

Zu Ihrer weiteren Information[2] finden Sie in der Anlage einen detaillierten Lebenslauf. Ich würde mich freuen, bald von Ihnen zu hören.

Mit besten Grüßen

R. Binder

<u>Anlage</u>
Lebenslauf

1 *Um ein Vierfaches*: lit. 'fourfold'. Note also *um ein Dreifaches*; *um ein Fünffaches*, etc.
2 *Zu Ihrer weiteren Information*: 'for your further information'. Note the preposition used.

31 Interview invitation

Ms F Jones
23 Park View
Colchester
Essex CO4 3RN

Dear Ms Jones

Ref. PS/2021: Personnel assistant

Interviews for the above position will take place on Friday, 22 February 199-, beginning at 10 a.m.

We expect to conclude the interviews after lunch, at approximately 2.30 p.m.

Please confirm whether you will be able to attend the interview.

Yours sincerely

Mr C Smith
Personnel Officer

31 Einladung zum Vorstellungsgespräch

Frau
Johanna Richter
Am Park 17

4020 Linz

Betr: Chefsekretärin – Zeichen PS/2021

Sehr geehrte Frau Richter,

Vorstellungsgespräche für die obige Stellung finden am Freitag, 22. Februar 199-
um 10.00 Uhr statt.

Ende der Interviews voraussichtlich um 14.30 Uhr.

Bitte bestätigen Sie Ihre Teilnahme.

Mit besten Grüßen

S. Schmidt
Personalleiter

32 Favourable reply to job application

Mrs L Flint
7 Fisherman's Way
Okehampton
Devon EX12 0YX

Dear Mrs Flint

I am writing to offer you formally the position of personal assistant to the operations director at Farnbury.

As discussed at the interview the normal working hours are 8.30 a.m.–5 p.m., Monday to Friday, although the position requires a flexible approach and on occasions you will be expected to work outside these times. The annual salary is £18,000.

You will receive further details if you accept the position.

Please confirm in writing by first post, Monday 3 April at the latest, whether you accept the offer of the position.

Yours sincerely

32 Positive Antwort auf Bewerbung

Frau Laura Feuerstein
Fischergasse 56

27000 Bremen

Sehr geehrte Frau Feuerstein,

Wir möchten Ihnen hiermit offiziell die Stellung als Chefsekretärin unseres Betriebsleiters in Bremerhaven anbieten.

Wie bereits beim Vorstellungsgespräch erwähnt ist die normale Arbeitszeit 8.30 Uhr – 17.00 Uhr, montags bis freitags, doch da Ihre Position eine gewisse Flexibilität erfordert, wird erwartet, daß Sie gelegentlich außerhalb dieser Zeit tätig sind. Ihr Gehalt beträgt monatlich DM 3450.

Weitere Einzelheiten erhalten Sie, wenn Sie die Stellung angenommen haben.

Bitte schicken Sie uns umgehend, spätestens aber bis Montag, 3. April, Ihre schriftliche Bestätigung, ob Sie unser Angebot annehmen.

Mit freundlichen Grüßen

L. Kenner

33 Unfavourable reply to job application

Mr R Smith
15 Adams Way
Reading
Berks
RG23 6WD

Dear Mr Smith

RE: POSITION AS SALES DIRECTOR

I am writing to inform you that your application was unsuccessful on this occasion.

I thank you for your interest in our company and wish you every success with your career.

Yours sincerely

33 Negative Antwort auf Bewerbung

Herrn
Robert Reiter
Adamgasse 15

28794 Cuxhaven

Sehr geehrter Herr Reiter,

wir möchten Ihnen mitteilen, daß Sie mit Ihrer Bewerbung dieses Mal keinen Erfolg hatten.

Vielen Dank für Ihr Interesse an unserem Unternehmen und unsere besten Wünsche für eine erfolgreiche Berufslaufbahn.[1]

Mit freundlichen Grüßen

L. Kenner

1 *Berufslaufbahn*: 'career'. Also possible: *Karriere*.

34　Requesting a reference for an applicant

Your ref. AS/
Our ref. FG/JL

2 February 199-

The Manager
First Class Bank
1–6, King's Square
BURY

Dear Mr Swift

RE: MISS STEPHANIE BOSSOM

This branch of the Safety First has recently received an application for employment as an accounts clerk from Ms Stephanie Bossom, who has quoted your name as a referee to whom we might address ourselves in the event of our wishing to interview her.

I believe that Ms Bossom has been working in your bank for several years and that her desire to change employment is prompted largely by her intention to marry and settle in this area. From her application it would seem that she would be a valuable asset to us; therefore we should be most grateful if you could confirm our impression in writing (by fax if possible) as soon as is convenient.

Please feel free to comment on any aspect of Ms Bossom's work that you deem to be of likely interest to us.

I thank you in advance for your co-operation.

Yours sincerely

Frank Graham
Branch Manager

34 Ersuchen um Bewerberreferenz

2. Februar 199-

PRIMA Bank
z.H. Herrn F. Rasch
Königsallee 1–6

40000 Düsseldorf

Ihre Zeichen: AS/   Unsere Zeichen: FG/JL

Sehr geehrter Herr Rasch,

die hiesige TOTAL Zweigstelle hat vor kurzem ein Bewerbungsschreiben von Frau Stefanie Bessemer erhalten. Frau Bessemer bewirbt sich um die Stelle als Mitarbeiterin in der Buchhaltung und hat Ihren Namen als Referenz angegeben,[1] sollten wir sie zu einem Einstellungsgespräch einladen.

Soviel ich weiß, war Frau Bessemer einige Jahre in Ihrer Bank beschäftigt, und ihr beabsichtigter Stellungswechsel rührt daher, daß sie nach ihrer Heirat in unserem Gebiet ihren Wohnsitz nehmen möchte.

Ihrer Bewerbung nach scheint es, daß sie für uns eine Bereicherung bedeuten könnte. Wir wären daher äußerst dankbar, wenn Sie uns Ihre Eindrücke so bald wie möglich schriftlich oder per Fax übermitteln könnten.

Bitte kommentieren Sie uneingeschränkt alle Aspekte von Frau Bessemers Tätigkeit, die Ihrer Meinung nach für uns von Interesse wären.

Ich darf Ihnen bereits im voraus für Ihr Entgegenkommen vielmals danken.

Mit besten Grüßen

Franz Gruber

1 *Als Referenz*: 'as referee'.

35 Providing a positive reference for an employee

4 February 199-

Your ref. FG/JL
Our ref. AS/MN

Mr F Graham
Safety First Assurance plc
12 Bright Street
Lancaster

Dear Mr Graham

MS STEPHANIE BOSSOM

I hasten to reply to your request for a reference for Ms. Stephanie Bossom. Please accept my apologies for not being able to fax my reply, but at present we are experiencing problems with the machine.

Yes, Stephanie has been an ideal employee who started with us as an office junior straight from school and has been promoted on several occasions in recognition of her work. I understand her reasons for wishing to leave; had she stayed, I would very soon have been promoting her myself.

You will see from her application that she has sat and passed a number of professional examinations over the last two years. In that time she has taken responsibility for supervising the progress of trainees and has been involved in new initiatives relating to our office systems.

You will find Stephanie a pleasant, willing and talented person who can be relied upon in the carrying out of her professional duties to the best of her ability at all times.

I hope you will be able to offer her the post, which you imply is likely in your initial letter.

Yours sincerely

Alan Swift
Manager, Town Centre Branch

35 Positive Referenz

4. Februar 199-

TOTAL Versicherung GmbH
z.H. Herrn F. Gruber
Stadtplatz 12a

88400 Konstanz

Ihr Zeichen: FG/JL
Unser Zeichen: AR/MN

Sehr geehrter Herr Gruber,

umgehend komme ich gerne Ihrem Ersuchen um eine Referenz für Frau Stefanie
Bessemer nach. Bitte entschuldigen Sie, daß ich meine Antwort nicht per Fax
übermitteln kann, da wir zur Zeit Schwierigkeiten mit unserem Gerät haben.

Stefanie ist tatsächlich eine ausgezeichnete Mitarbeiterin. Sie kam zu uns direkt
von der Schule und begann als Bürolehrling. In Anerkennung ihrer Leistung
wurde sie mehrmals befördert. Ich verstehe die Gründe, warum sie unsere
Organisation verlassen möchte. Wäre sie geblieben, hätte ich sie in nächster Zeit
selbst befördert.[1]

Aus ihrer Bewerbung werden Sie entnehmen, daß sie während der letzten beiden
Jahre verschiedene Fachprüfungen erfolgreich abgelegt hat.[2] In dieser Zeit
übernahm sie auch die Verantwortung für die Fortschrittskontrolle des
Trainingsprogramms. Sie war auch mitbeteiligt an büropraktischen Initiativen.

Sie werden in Stefanie eine freundliche, bereitwillige und begabte Mitarbeiterin
finden, welche die ihr gestellten fachlichen Aufgaben jederzeit tüchtig und
verläßlich ausführen wird.

Ich hoffe, daß Sie, wie in Ihrem Brief angedeutet, in der Lage sein werden, ihr die
Stellung zum Angebot zu machen.

Mit besten Grüßen

Andreas Rasch
Filialleiter

1 *Wäre sie geblieben ...*: this avoids the use of *wenn ...* with the subsequent change of
   word order.
2 *Eine Prüfung ablegen*: 'to take an examination'. *Eine Prüfung bestehen*: 'to pass an
   examination'. *Bei der Prüfung durchfallen*: 'to fail the exam'.

36 Acceptance letter

Melton's Motor Factors Ltd
63 Station Road
Thirsk
N. Yorkshire
YO9 4YN

Dear Sir

Thank you for your letter of 17 July in which you offer me the post of parts manager.

I am delighted to inform you that I accept your offer.

Yours sincerely

W Holland

36 Annahme eines Stellenangebots

WV Motorwerke
Bahnhofstr. 17–20

01653 Meißen

Sehr geehrte Damen und Herren,

ich danke Ihnen für Ihren Brief vom 17. Juli, in dem Sie mir die Stellung des Leiters der Abteilung Ersatzteile anbieten.

Ich freue mich, Ihnen mitteilen zu können, daß ich Ihr Angebot gerne annehme.

Mit besten Grüßen

W. Hofer

37 Contract of employment

Dear

Following recent discussions we are pleased to offer you employment at our Company as Area Manager on the following terms and conditions:-

Remuneration
Your salary will be £15,000 per annum plus commission on the basis we have already discussed with you. As with all our staff your salary will be paid monthly on the last Thursday in each month, your first review being in July 199-.

Notice
As with all our staff, you will be employed for an initial trial period of six months, during which time either you or we may terminate your appointment at any time upon giving seven days' notice in writing to the other. Provided that we are satisfied with your performance during the trial period, we will thereafter immediately confirm your appointment as a permanent member of our staff and the seven days' period of notice referred to above will be increased to one month.

Sickness Pay
During any reasonable absence for illness the Company, at its discretion, will make up the amount of your National Insurance Benefit to the equivalent of your normal salary, although this will be essentially relative to your length of service.

Holidays
Your normal paid holiday entitlement will be 20 working days in a full year, the holiday year running from 1 January to 31 December.

Car
We will provide you with a suitable Company car (cost circa £14,000), which is to be mainly for your business use but also for your private use. The Company will meet all normal running expenses associated with the car such as road tax, insurance, repairs, servicing and petrol.

Pensions
The Company operates its own Pension Plan. You can either decide to join the Company Scheme after six months' service at the Scheme's next anniversary date (July 199-), or alternatively choose a Personal Pension Plan to which the Company would contribute.

Hours
Normal office hours are from 9.00 a.m. to 5.15 p.m. from Monday to Friday with one hour for lunch. However, it is probable that additional calls will be made upon your time.

37 Arbeitsvertrag

Sehr geehrter Herr/geehrte Frau_____

im Anschluß an unser kürzliches Gespräch freuen wir uns, Ihnen die Stellung als Regionalleiter zu den folgenden Bedingungen anbieten zu können:

Vergütung
Ihr Jahresgehalt beträgt 34500 DM sowie Provision auf der von uns bereits erörterten Basis. Die Auszahlung erfolgt wie für unsere ganze Belegschaft monatlich u. zw.[1] am letzten Donnerstag des Monats. Ihre erste Gehaltserhöhung wird im Juli 199- stattfinden.

Kündigung
Wie für unsere ganze Belegschaft gilt für Sie eine anfängliche Probezeit von sechs Monaten, während dieser eine beiderseitige Aufkündigung des Anstellungsverhältnisses jederzeit binnen sieben Tagen schriftlich erfolgen kann. Vorausgesetzt Ihre Probezeit verlief zu unserer Zufriedenheit, werden wir Ihre Festanstellung unmittelbar danach bestätigen. Die Kündigungsfrist wird sich in diesem Falle von sieben Tagen auf einen Monat verlängern.[2]

Krankengeld
Während berechtigter Abwesenheit aus Krankheitsgründen wird die Firma nach eigenem Ermessen die Krankenversicherungsbeiträge auf Ihr Gehaltsniveau ausgleichen. Dies wird aber im wesentlichen von der Zahl Ihrer Dienstjahre abhängen.

Urlaub
Ihr Anspruch auf bezahlten Urlaub beträgt normalerweise 20 Arbeitstage pro Jahr, mit Beginn am 1. Januar und Ende am 31. Dezember.

Firmenwagen
Wir stellen Ihnen einen geeigneten Firmenwagen (Kosten etwa 32000 DM) hauptsächlich für geschäftliche Zwecke aber auch für Ihren privaten Gebrauch zur Verfügung. Für die üblichen Betriebskosten wie Straßenbenützungsgebühr, Versicherung, Reparatur, Wartung und Treibstoff, werden wir aufkommen.

Altersversorgung
Die Firma hat ihren eigenen Altersversorgungsplan. Es steht Ihnen frei, der betrieblichen Rentenversicherung nach sechsmonatiger Dienstzeit zum nächsten Jahrestermin beizutreten oder einen privaten Pensionsplan zu wählen, zu dem die Firma Beitrag leistet.

Arbeitszeit
Normale Dienstzeit ist von 09.00–17.15 Uhr von Montag bis Freitag mit einer Stunde Mittagspause. Es ist aber durchaus möglich, daß Ihre Zeit zusätzlich in Anspruch genommen werden kann.

Grievance and Disciplinary Procedure

Should you wish to seek redress for any grievance relating to your employment, you should refer, as appropriate, either to the Company Secretary or to the Managing Director. Matters involving discipline will be dealt with in as fair and equitable a manner as possible.

Health & Safety at Work Act

A copy of the Staff Notice issued under the Health & Safety at Work Act 1974 will be given to you on the first day of your employment. Your acceptance of the appointment will be deemed to constitute your willingness to comply with these regulations.

Start Date

The date on which your employment by the Company is to commence remains to be agreed by us. We look forward to establishing a mutually acceptable date as soon as possible.

Will you kindly provide us with your acceptance of this offer of employment by signing and returning to us the enclosed duplicate copy of this letter.

We trust that you will have a long, happy and successful association with our Company.

Yours sincerely

B. Foster
Managing Director

Enc.

Beschwerde- und Disziplinarweg

Zur Bereinigung einer Beschwerdesituation sollten Sie sich entsprechend entweder an den Prokuristen oder an den Geschäftsführer wenden. Disziplinäre Angelegenheiten werden so gerecht und unparteilich wie möglich behandelt.

Arbeitsschutzvorschriften

Bei Dienstantritt erhalten Sie eine Belegschaftsmitteilung, ausgegeben im Zusammenhang mit dem Arbeitschutzgesetz von 1974. Ihre Annahme der Stellung gilt als Bereitschaft, diese Vorschriften einzuhalten.[3]

Beginn Ihrer Tätigkeit

Die Entscheidung über das Datum Ihres Arbeitsantritts bleibt der Firma vorbehalten. Wir hoffen, einen beiderseits geeigneten Zeitpunkt so bald wie möglich festzusetzen.

Zur Annahme unseres Stellenangebots wären wir Ihnen dankbar, wenn Sie die beiliegende Kopie dieses Briefes unterschrieben an uns zurücksenden würden.

Wir hoffen auf eine lange, glückliche und erfolgreiche Zusammenarbeit mit Ihnen.

Mit besten Grüßen

B. Förster
Geschäftsführer

Anlage
Kopie

1 *U. zw.*: 'und zwar'.
2 *Verlängern auf*: 'extend to'. Similarly *erhöhen auf*: 'increase to'.
3 *Vorschriften einhalten*: 'respect/keep to the regulations'. Also *einen Termin einhalten*: 'make/keep an appointment'.

38 Enquiring about regulations for purchase of property abroad (memo)

LUJIPROP SA

Internal memorandum

From: Terry Baddison (Customer Services)
To: Guillermo Estuardos (Legal Department)

Date: 9 September 199-

Message: I urgently need some information on current rules and regulations
            concerning the purchase and renting of property in Spain. We have
            some clients interested in the new complex at Carboneras, but we
            are not sure whether they can sublet part of the premises without
            paying local tax on the rental. Can you check this out ASAP?

            P.S. I'm in the office every afternoon this week.

            Terry

38 Anfrage über Vorschriften bezügl.[1] Immobilienkauf im Ausland (Mitteilung)

Hausmitteilung

Von: Herrn T. Petersen (Kundendienst)
An: Herrn G. Estuardos (Rechtsabteilung)

Datum: 09.09.9-

Ich brauche dringend Informationen über die derzeit gültigen Vorschriften und Bestimmungen betreffs Ankauf oder Miete spanischer Immobilien. Einige Kunden haben Interesse an der neuen Anlage in Carboneras, aber wir sind nicht sicher, ob sie Ortstaxe erlegen müssen, wenn sie die Räumlichkeiten weiter vermieten. Könnten Sie die Angelegenheit so bald wie möglich klären?

P.S. Ich bin die ganze Woche nachmittags im Hause.

T.

1 *Bezügl.*: abbreviation for *bezüglich*: 'concerning', 'regarding'.

39 Advising of delay in delivery (telex)

TELEX: Expofrut (Almería, Spain) to Henshaw Bros. (Wolverhampton, England)

Subject: Delay in delivery

Sender: Pablo López
Addressee: Mary Henshaw
Date: 1 May 199-

Message: APOLOGIES FOR FAILING TO DELIVER USUAL ORDER THIS WEEK.

DOCKS STRIKE CALLED FROM TODAY THROUGHOUT SPAIN.

YOUR CONSIGNMENT OF FRUIT AND VEGETABLES ON QUAYSIDE. STILL POSSIBLE TO SEND GOODS BY ROAD, BUT COULD NOT GUARANTEE DELIVERY BY WEEKEND.

INFORM BY TELEPHONE (00 3451 947583) THIS P.M. IF TO PROCEED WITH ORDER BY ROAD.

REGARDS

Pablo López
(Export Manager)

39 Mitteilung über Lieferverzögerung (Fernschreiben)

TELEX: Expofrut (Almeria, Spanien)

           An
           Gebrüder Sievers (Bremen, Deutschland)

Betrifft: Lieferverzögerung

Absender: Pablo López
Adressat: Martin Sievers
Datum: 1. Mai 199-

Nachricht: Bedauern Ausfall der normalen Lieferung diese Woche.
            Hafenarbeiterstreik heute für ganz Spanien ausgerufen.
            Ihre Obst- und Gemüseladung z.Zt. im Hafen.[1] Möglichkeit des
            Straßentransports, aber keine Garantie, daß Lieferung bis
            Wochenende eintrifft. Bitte um Telefonbescheid (00 3451 947583)
            heute nachmittag wegen Straßentransport.

            MfG[2]
            Pablo López

1   *Z. Zt.*: *zur Zeit.*
2   *MfG*: abbreviation for *mit freundlichen Grüßen.*

40 Seeking clarification of financial position (fax)

To: Accounts Section, MULTIBANK,
Prince's Square, Crewe

From: John Turket, PERLOANS
High Street, Tamworth

Date: 4 November 199-

No. of pages, including this: 2

Dear Sir

This company has been approached today by a Mr Alan Thomas, who wishes to secure a loan in order to finance a family visit to relatives living overseas. He has given his approval to my contacting your branch of Multibank, where he holds two accounts, in order to verify and clarify information he has proffered about his financial position.

Once you have satisfied yourselves that Mr Thomas is willing that you divulge facts about his finances, can you please provide the following information?

1 Has Mr Thomas incurred major overdrafts since 1990?

2 Do both Mr Thomas and his wife have salary cheques paid directly each month Into their current account?

3 Does your bank have any reason to believe that Mr Thomas will not be able to repay a £3,000 loan to Perloans over 3 years from July 199-.

We hope you feel able to respond to our request, and thank you for your assistance in this matter.

Yours faithfully

John Turket
Loans Manager

40 Einholung einer Bankreferenz (Fax)

An: Kontenabteilung, Oberbank
             Fürstenplatz, 86345 Augsburg

Von: Walter Türk, Kreditverleih FAMILIA
             Hauptstr. 34, Nürnberg.

Datum: 4. November 199-

Sehr geehrte Herren,

in einem Schreiben an unser Unternehmen bewirbt sich Herr Andreas Thomas um einen Kredit zur Finanzierung einer Reise, um mit seiner Familie Verwandte in Übersee zu besuchen. Er gab mir die Erlaubnis, mich mit Ihrer Filiale, bei der er Inhaber zweier Konten ist,[1] in Verbindung zu setzen, um seine eigene Auskunft über seine Finanzlage zu überprüfen.

Sobald Sie selbst Herrn Thomases Zustimmung zu Ihrer Auskunftserteilung eingeholt haben, wären wir Ihnen dankbar für die folgenden Informationen:

1. Hat Herr Thomas seine Konten seit 1990 in größerem Maße überzogen?

2. Werden die Monatsgehälter von Herrn Thomas sowie seiner Frau direkt auf ihre laufenden Konten überwiesen?

3. Hat Ihre Bank Grund zur Annahme, daß Herr Thomas nicht in der Lage ist, eine Anleihe von 6500 DM innerhalb von drei Jahren beginnend im Juli 199- zurückzuerstatten?

Wir hoffen, daß Sie in der Lage sind, unserem Ersuchen nachzukommen, und danken Ihnen für Ihre Hilfe in dieser Angelegenheit.

Mit besten Grüßen

Walter Türk
Leitung Kreditabteilung

1 *Zweier Konten*: this is very formal style. *Von zwei Konten* is less elevated.
2 *Innerhalb von drei Jahren*: *innerhalb* is used with the genitive if the genitive case can be indicated by an appropriate ending (*innerhalb einer Woche*). If not, then it is used with the dative, as here.

41 Reporting to client on availability of particular property (fax)

To: Ms L Topcopy
            Trendset Printers

From: Mrs D Russell
            Smith & Jones

Date: 6 September 199-

No. of pages, including this: 1

Re: Office for lease

Dear Ms Topcopy

I am faxing you urgently to let you know that office premises have just become available in the area of town you said you liked. The lease on a street-front shop with an office on the first floor has been cancelled early by another client who is moving south. If you would like to see the property, please get back to us this afternoon and we will arrange a visit.

Best wishes

Dorothy Russell

41 Kundeninformation bezügl. Bürovermietung (Fax)

An: Frau L. Gutenberg
        Druck 2000

Von: Frau D. Rüßler
        Zimmer & Frahm

Datum: 06.09.9-

Betrifft: Bürovermietung

Sehr geehrte Frau Gutenberg,

ich möchte Ihnen dringend mitteilen, daß Büroräume in dem von Ihnen bevorzugten Stadtteil verfügbar wurden. Einer unserer Kunden hat wegen seines beabsichtigten Umzugs nach Süddeutschland die Miete eines straßenseitig gelegenen Geschäftes mit Büro im 1. Stock vorzeitig gekündigt. Sollten Sie die Liegenschaft sehen wollen, bitte setzen Sie sich noch diesen Nachmittag mit uns in Verbindung, und wir vereinbaren eine Besichtigung.

MfG

D. Rüßler

42 Complaining about customs delay (fax)

To: HM Customs and Excise
                London

From: Ordenasa, Madrid

Date: 21/2/9-

No. of pages: 1

Dear Sirs

On behalf of my director colleagues of this computer software business I wish to lodge a complaint about customs clearance at British airports.

On several occasions since October 199- materials freighted from Madrid to retailers in Great Britain have been subject to unexplained and unjustifiable delays. This company depends for success on its ability to respond quickly to market demand; furthermore, at all times the requisite export licences have been in order.

This communication by fax is prompted by the latest and most frustrating hold-up, at Gatwick Airport yesterday, which has allowed a market competitor to secure a valuable contract ahead of us.

If the Single Market is to function effectively this is precisely the type of situation that must be avoided. I intend to contact the relevant Chamber of Commerce, but in the meantime I insist on an explanation from your officers of why consignment AT/463 was not permitted immediate entry on 20 February 199-.

Yours faithfully

Dr. Norberto Mateos
(Managing Director)

42 Beschwerde über Zollprobleme (Fax)

An: Deutsche Zollbehörde, Frankfurt

Von: ORDENASA, Madrid

Datum: 21.02.9-

Sehr geehrte Damen und Herren,

im Namen meiner Vorstandskollegen im obigen Computer Software Unternehmen möchte ich mich über die Zollabfertigung am Frankfurter Flughafen beschweren.

Seit Oktober 199- wurden unsere per Luftfracht aus Madrid angelieferten Waren mehrmals unerklärlichen wie auch ungerechtfertigten Verzögerungen ausgesetzt.

Der Erfolg unserer Firma hängt von einem raschen Reagieren auf die Bedürfnisse des Marktes ab; noch dazu entsprachen die erforderlichen Einfuhrgenehmigungen zu jeder Zeit den geltenden Bestimmungen.

Diese Fax-Mitteilung ist eine Reaktion auf die jüngste und äußerst frustrierende gestrige Verzögerung am Frankfurter Flughafen, was einem Konkurrenzunternehmen einen bedeutenden Vorsprung bei einem Geschäftsabschluß zusicherte.

Zur reibungslosen Abwicklung des Gemeinsamen Binnenmarktes[1] sollten Situationen wie diese tunlichst vermieden werden.

Ich beabsichtige auch, mich an die zuständige Handelskammer zu wenden, doch inzwischen muß ich auf einer offiziellen Erklärung darüber bestehen, warum der Lieferung AT/463 am 20. Februar die direkte Einreise verweigert wurde.

Hochachtungsvoll

Dr. Norberto Mateos
Geschäftsführer

1 *Binnenmarkt* (here): Single Market. It can also be used to mean simply 'domestic market'.

43 Stating delivery conditions

1 August 199-

Your Reference: AD/LR
Our Reference: TH/PA

Sr José Escalante
Managing Director
Escalante e Hijos
Avenida del Sol
San Sebastián
SPAIN

Dear Mr Escalante

Thank you for your fax communication of yesterday regarding the delivery of the chickens and other poultry ordered by you from this company in early July. As we indicated in our original quote to Mr Salas, who first contacted us, the delivery can only be guaranteed if your bank is able to confirm that debts owed to us will be cleared this week.

Please note that our drivers would much appreciate assistance with overnight accommodation and that any costs they incur should be charged directly to Bridge Farm on completion of the delivery next week.

We look forward to hearing from you on both matters.

Yours sincerely

Tom Holbrook
Transport Manager

43 Versandbedingungen

1. August 199-

IDAL
z.H. Herrn W. Ecker, Geschäftsführer
Sonnenweg 28

D–25041 Kiel

Sehr geehrter Herr Ecker,

besten Dank für Ihre gestrige Faxmitteilung bezüglich der Hühner- und
Geflügellieferung, die Sie bei uns Anfang Juli bestellt haben.[1] Wie wir bereits
Herrn Stiller, unserem ersten Kontakt mit Ihnen, in unserer ursprünglichen
Preisangabe bedeutet haben, können wir die Lieferung nur dann gewährleisten,
wenn Ihre Bank noch diese Woche die Begleichung unserer Forderungen
bestätigen kann.

Dürften wir Sie auch ersuchen, bei der Beschaffung von
Übernachtungsgelegenheiten für unsere Transportfahrer behilflich zu sein, wobei
alle in diesem Zusammenhang entstandenen Unkosten uns direkt nach
Ausführung der Lieferung nächste Woche in Rechnung zu stellen sind.

Wir freuen uns, von Ihnen in beiden Angelegenheiten zu hören.

Mit besten Grüßen

Tom Holbrook
Transportleiter

---

1 *Anfang Juli*: 'at the beginning of July'. When used in the temporal sense, *Anfang* does
not require a preposition (cf: *Mitte Mai, Ende Oktober*, but *am Ende der Straße*).

44 Confirming time/place of delivery

12 June 199-

Your Reference: RCG/LP
Our Reference: FG/JD

Dr Rosa Castro Giménez
Subdirectora
Departamento de Relaciones Exteriores
Ministerio de Industria
Quito
ECUADOR

Dear Madam

Further to our communication of 9 May in which we outlined to your department the likely oil needs of the companies we represent, it is with some concern that we have heard indirectly that your Ministry may be unable to fulfil its immediate responsibilities. We would be most obliged to hear, at your earliest convenience, that the draft agreement signed recently by our representatives remains valid.

In spite of our concern we are fully committed to the trading relations discussed and as such wish to confirm details of first delivery of manufactured goods being exchanged for the above-mentioned oil imports. Carlton Excavators plc have confirmed this week that the consignment of earthmovers, tractors and diggers bound for Constructores Velasco was loaded on Monday of this week. The consignment should reach the port of Guayaquil by the end of the month. We will, of course, provide you with more precise details nearer the time.

Meanwhile, please accept our best wishes for the continuation of our collaborative venture as we await your confirmation regarding the deliveries of your oil to our New South Wales terminal.

Yours faithfully

Frank Gardner
Senior Partner

44 Versandbestätigung

12. Juni 199-

Dr. Rosa Castro Gimnez
Subdirectora
Departamento de Relaciones Exteriores
Ministerio de Industria
Quito
Ecuador

Sehr geehrte Frau Dr. Castro Giménez,

wir beziehen uns auf unser Schreiben an Ihre Abteilung vom 9. Mai, in dem wir den erwarteten Ölbedarf der von uns vertretenen Unternehmen kurz darlegten. Zu unserer Besorgnis hören wir nun von anderer Seite, daß Ihr Ministerium möglicherweise nicht in der Lage ist, seinen direkten Verpflichtungen nachzukommen. Wir wären Ihnen daher äußerst dankbar, wenn Sie uns so bald wie möglich mitteilen könnten, ob der von Ihren Vertretern kürzlich unterzeichnete Vertragsentwurf weiterhin gültig bleibt.

Trotz unserer Besorgnis möchten wir unseren Einsatz für die abgesprochenen Handelsbeziehungen betonen und in diesem Zusammenhang die Einzelheiten des Versandes von Fertigprodukten im Austausch für obig erwähnte Ölimporte bestätigen.

Karlsson Baumaschinen GmbH haben diese Woche die Verschiffung einer Ladung von Traktoren, Baggern und anderen Maschinen zur Erdbewegung am Montag an die Firma Constructores Velasco bestätigt. Die Ladung wird den Hafen von Guayaquil voraussichtlich am Ende des Monats erreichen. Wir werden Ihnen selbstverständlich vorher noch genauere Einzelheiten zukommen lassen.

In der Zwischenzeit erwarten wir Ihre Bestätigung in bezug auf Ihre Öllieferung nach Hamburg und geben unseren Wünschen für die Fortdauer unserer gemeinsamen Unternehmungen Ausdruck.

Mit besten Grüßen

Friedrich Gärtner
Seniorpartner

45 Checking on mode of transportation

19 February 19-

Your ref. SM/MB
Our ref. TS/PU

Mr Sebastián Morán
Sales Manager
Hermanos García SA
Carretera Luis Vargas, 24
CUENCA
Spain

Dear Mr Morán

Thank you for your letter sent on Tuesday last in which you refer to the kitchen equipment we ordered from García Brothers in December. As you know, our market has been rather depressed, but there are recent signs of improvement, and as a result we now need to receive the cupboard doors and worktops much more promptly than hitherto.

Can you please confirm that where necessary you would be able to deliver some items by road, or even by air if very urgent, rather than by the sea route you currently use?

We have checked that from Valencia it would be possible to airfreight at a reasonable price to East Midlands Airport on a Monday afternoon and a Thursday evening.

I would be grateful if you could send us a reply confirming whether our proposal is viable.

Yours sincerely

Trevor Sharp
Warehouse Manager

45 Transportmittel

19. Februar 199-

Hager Küchen
z.H. Herrn S. Mann, Verkaufsleiter
Postfach 275

D 31856 Hannover

Sehr geehrter Herr Mann,

besten Dank für Ihren Brief vom letzten Dienstag bezüglich der von uns bei Ihnen im Dezember bestellten Kücheneinrichtungen. Wie Sie wissen, ist die Marktsituation bei uns zur Zeit noch ziemlich flau,[1] doch jüngsten Anzeichen von Erholung zufolge liegt uns daran, die Schranktüren und Arbeitsflächen pünktlicher als bisher zu erhalten.

Könnten Sie uns bitte verbindlich zusagen, daß Sie bei Bedarf bestimmte Artikel auf dem Landweg oder im dringenden Falle sogar auf dem Luftweg statt auf dem derzeit benützten Seeweg befördern könnten?

Unseres Wissens[2] gibt es jeden Montag nachmittag und jeden Donnerstag abend eine preisgünstige Luftfrachtverbindung von Hamburg zum Flughafen East Midlands.

Ich wäre Ihnen dankbar für Ihre Antwort, sollten Sie unsere Vorschläge annehmbar finden.

Mit freundlichen Grüßen

Trevor Sharp
Lagerhausleiter

1 *Flau*: 'flat', 'dead', 'lifeless'. Note also: *die Flaute*: 'recession'.
2 *Unseres Wissens*: this is very formal. *Wir glauben* ... would be just as acceptable.

46 Claiming for transportation damage

Claims Department
Lifeguard Assurance plc
Safeside House
High Street
Bromsgove
Worcs.

Dear Sir/Madam

POLICY NO. AL 78/2139B

My letter concerns a claim I wish to make on behalf of this firm, Anchor Lighting. We have had a policy with your company for many years, and rarely have needed to call upon your services. This time, however, we have suffered a serious financial loss due to damage incurred during the transit of goods.

Last week a whole consignment of lamps and other fittings was lost when our delivery truck ran off the road and turned over. The retail value of the merchandise ruined was in the region of £7,000, a sum equivalent to an entire quarter's profit.

I would be most grateful if you could send at your earliest convenience a major claim form and some general information on your settlement procedures.

Our policy number is as follows: AL 78/2139B.

I look forward to hearing from you soon.

Yours faithfully

Brian Tomkinson
Proprietor

46 Schadenersatzforderung für Transport

Adler Versicherung Gmbh
Luegerring 14/II

1010 Wien

Sehr geehrte Damen und Herren,

ich beziehe mich in meinem Schreiben auf einen Antrag auf Schadenersatz, den ich im Namen der Firma Anker Beleuchtungshaus stellen möchte. Wir haben seit Jahren einen Versicherungsvertrag mit Ihrer Gesellschaft und hatten nur wenig Anlaß, Ihre Dienste in Anspruch zu nehmen. Diesmal aber erlitten wir ernsthafte finanzielle Verluste aufgrund von Beschädigung unserer Waren beim Transport.

Eine gesamte Ladung von Lampen und anderen Beleuchtungskörpern wurde letzte Woche zerstört, als unser Lieferwagen von der Straße abkam und umstürzte. Der Verkaufswert der nun unbrauchbaren Waren belief sich auf 700 000, -S, was dem Gewinn eines ganzen Quartals entspricht.

Bitte schicken Sie so bald wie möglich ein Antragsformular sowie allgemeine Informationen über Ihr Auszahlungsverfahren.

Unsere Versicherungspolizze hat die Nummer AL 78/21398.

Ich würde mich freuen, bald von Ihnen zu hören.

Mit besten Grüßen

Andreas Hofer
Inhaber

47 Enquiring about customs clearance

5 November 199-

Your ref.
Our ref. TC/LJ

The Customs and Excise Branch
Chilean Trade Ministry
SANTIAGO
Chile
South America

Dear Sirs

I have been advised to write to you directly by the Commercial Section of the Chilean Embassy in London. My company produces high-tech toys for the world market. At a recent trade fair in Barcelona several Chilean retailers expressed interest in importing our products. They were, however, unable to provide information on customs formalities in your country. Similarly, the London Embassy has recommended that I consult your Branch to seek up-to-date information.

The situation is as follows: our products include computer games, remote-control toy cars and mini-sized televisions. It seems that goods made in the EU are subject to a customs process rather more restrictive than those from Japan or the USA. As my company is a wholly-owned subsidiary of a US parent firm, would it be easier and cheaper to export to Chile from the USA rather than from Britain?

Our intention is not merely to circumvent regulations but to optimize our operations at a time when such matters as customs clearance can result in costly delays.

We thank you for your attention and look forward to an early reply from you.

Yours sincerely

Thomas Carty
Managing Director

47 Erkundigung über Zollabfertigung

5 November 199-

An das
Handelsministerium der Republik Chile
Zollabteilung

Santiago
Chile

Sehr geehrte Damen und Herren,

auf Anraten der chilenischen Botschaft, Sektion Handel, richten wir unser Schreiben direkt an Sie. Wir sind Hersteller von High-Tech-Spielzeug für den Weltmarkt. Auf einer Messe in Barcelona zeigten sich unlängst einige chilenische Einzelhändler sehr interessiert an einer Einfuhr unserer Waren. Leider aber waren sie nicht in der Lage, Auskunft über die Zollformalitäten Ihres Landes zu geben, ähnlich wie die Botschaft in Bonn, die uns daher empfahl, Sie um Auskunft über den neuesten Stand der Dinge zu ersuchen.

Es handelt sich um folgende Situation: Wir führen unter anderem Computerspiele, Spielzeugautos mit Fernsteuerung und Miniatur-Fernsehapparate. Dem Anschein nach sind Erzeugnisse der Europäischen Union einem strengeren Zollverfahren unterworfen als die aus Japan oder den USA.[1] Da unser Betrieb die Tochterfirma[2] im Alleinbesitz eines US-Unternehmens ist, möchten wir gerne wissen, ob der Export nach Chile aus den Vereinigten Staaten problemloser und billiger als aus der Bundesrepublik wäre.

Es liegt uns nicht so sehr an der Umgehung von Bestimmungen, sondern an einer bestmöglichen Abwicklung unserer Geschäfte unter Vermeidung von kostspieligen Verzögerungen in der Zollabfertigung.

Wir wären Ihnen dankbar, wenn Sie diesem Sachverhalt Ihre Aufmerksamkeit schenken würden, und freuen uns, bald von Ihnen zu hören.

Mit besten Grüßen

Thomas Kettner
Geschäftsleiter

1 Note the construction *aus den USA*; because USA is plural.
2 *Tochterfirma*: 'subsidiary company'. Similarly, *Muttergesellschaft*: 'parent company'.

48 Undertaking customs formalities

27 November 199-

Your ref.
Our ref. RM/AP

HM Customs and Excise
Government Offices
LONDON WC2

Dear Sir/Madam

I write to inform you of a business operation in which my company is to be involved for the first time and to request your advice in the case of any misapprehension on my part.

As sole director of Leatherlux I have recently been able to conclude a deal with a firm of suppliers in Tunisia. I imagine that as a non-EU nation Tunisia cannot trade with complete freedom from import/export levies. I wish therefore to inform you that I intend to import from Nabeul in the next fortnight the following articles:

    150 men's leather jackets
     50 pairs of ladies' leather trousers
    250 leather belts
    100 pairs of leather sandals
     50 pairs of men's leather boots

I anticipate paying approximately £3,000 for the consignment. Can you please provide me with official documentation (if required) or at least confirm by fax that I shall be required to pay some form of duty on these imports?

I thank you in anticipation of your assistance.

Yours faithfully

Royston McAughey
Managing Director

48 Zollformalitäten

27. November 199-

An das Zollamt
Heinestr. 27

40002 Düsseldorf

Sehr geehrte Damen und Herren,

in Zusammenhang mit für meine Firma neuartigen geschäftlichen Unternehmungen möchte ich mich an Sie um Rat wenden,[1] um Mißverständnisse meinerseits möglichst zu vermeiden.

Als alleiniger Geschäftsleiter von Lederlux gelang mir kürzlich ein Geschäftsabschluß mit einer Lieferantenfirma in Tunesien. Da Tunesien als Nicht-EU-Land gewissen Ein- und Ausfuhrabgaben unterliegen dürfte, möchte ich Ihnen hiermit zur Kenntnis bringen, daß ich in den nächsten 14 Tagen folgende Artikel aus Nabeul zu importieren beabsichtige:

    150 Lederjacken für Herren
     50 Lederhosen für Damen
    250 Ledergürtel
    100 Paar Ledersandalen
     50 Lederstiefel für Herren

Der Preis für die Lieferung beträgt etwa 6900,- DM. Könnten Sie mir bitte nötigenfalls amtliche Papiere zukommen lassen oder zumindest möglichst per Fax bestätigen, daß ich gewisse Einfuhrabgaben zu entrichten habe.

Ich danke Ihnen im voraus für Ihre Hilfe und verbleibe

mit besten Grüßen

Richard Vandenhove
Geschäftsleiter

1 *Um Rat*: 'for advice'. Note the preposition.

49 Informing of storage facilities

13 June 199-

Your ref. JG/TK
Our ref. JS/PI

Hurd's (International) Removals
34–36, Wesley Avenue
CROYDON
Surrey

Dear Mrs Gordon

I am pleased to inform you that the container of household goods your company contracted us to transport from Australia has now been delivered to our depot here in Kent.

We will need by the end of this week to complete the official formalities, but you are welcome to pick up the unloaded contents for onward delivery to your customer from next Monday.

If you prefer to leave the goods here in store until further notice, please consult our price list (enclosed) for storage facilities and let us know your intention by fax.

As and when your driver does come to pick up the goods, he should enter the terminal by the side entrance which will lead him straight to the relevant loading area, marked DOMESTIC.

I trust these arrangements meet with your approval.

Yours sincerely

Jim Smith
Depot Manager

Enc.

49 Mitteilung zur Warenlagerung

13. Juni 199-

Spedition Hirt
z. H. Frau G. Jäger
Friesenweg 18-20

27456 Bremen

Sehr geehrte Frau Jäger,

wir freuen uns, Ihnen mitteilen zu können, daß der Container mit
Haushaltsgeräten, den wir im Auftrag Ihrer Firma aus Spanien beförderten, nun
in unserem Depot hier in Bremerhaven eingelangt ist.

Die amtlichen Formalitäten müssen bis zum Ende dieser Woche von uns erledigt
werden. Ab nächsten Montag können Sie dann die entladenen Waren zur
Weiterbeförderung an Ihre Kunden hier abholen.

Sollten Sie aber vorziehen, die Waren bis auf weiteres hier zu lagern, entnehmen
Sie bitte die Lagergebühren der beiliegenden Preisliste und faxen Sie uns Ihre
Mitteilung.

Zur Abholung der Waren sollte Ihr Fahrer den Seiteneingang zum
Kontainerterminal benutzen und direkt zum Ladebereich bezeichnet INLAND
weiterfahren.

Mit besten Grüßen

J. Schmidt
Depotleiter

Anlage
Preisliste

50 Assuring of confidentiality of information

1 November 199-

Your ref. EF/LJ
Our ref. HE/PI

Dr Ernesto Furillo
University Hospital
University of Managua
Managua
República de Nicaragua

Dear Dr Furillo

MISS ALICIA BARTOLOMÉ

Thank you for your letter of last month in which you sought confirmation that the reference you provided for Miss Alicia Bartolomé and her personal details would remain confidential.

It is the policy of the Government and of this Ministry to maintain total discretion when dealing with citizens from other countries who come here in order to develop their professional studies. Miss Bartolomé's course begins in three weeks' time. By then, her curriculum vitae will have been duly stored on computer in this Ministry and will be accessible only to those with the due authorization.

You may rest assured that all proper measures will be taken to protect the interests of our students.

Yours sincerely

Hortensia Enríquez Castro
Personnel Supervisor

50 Versicherung der Datengeheimhaltung

1. November 199-

Frau
Dr. E. F. Firth
University Hospital
University of Edinburgh

Edinburg
Großbritannien

Sehr geehrte Frau Dr. Firth,

wir danken Ihnen für Ihren Brief vom letzten Monat, in dem Sie uns ersuchen, die vertrauliche Behandlung Ihrer Referenz für Frl. Angela Bartholomew sowie ihrer persönlichen Daten zu bestätigen.

Der Datenschutz in bezug auf ausländische Studenten wird von unserer Universität grundsätzlich wahrgenommen. Die Vorlesungen für Frl. Bartholomews Studium beginnen in drei Wochen. Bis dahin wird ihr Lebenslauf im Universitätskomputer gespeichert und nur befugten Personen zugänglich sein.

Sie können also sicher sein, daß vollste Diskretion im Interesse unserer Studenten gewahrt bleibt.

Mit besten Grüßen

Dr. G. Radtner

51 Informing a client on conditions of loans/mortgages available

14 July 199-

Your ref. GB/LK
Our ref. PH/VE

Mr G Brookham
Managing Director
MultiCast
Floor 11
Forum House
Dukeries Avenue
Mansfield

Dear Mr Brookham

Since receiving your letter of 23 June we have been making enquiries on the matter of financing that you raised; please accept our apologies, nevertheless, for the delay. You will find enclosed three leaflets containing information about properties you may find interesting. We shall await your reaction to them.

More pressing, perhaps, is the question of finance. Having consulted local banks as well as our own finance broker, we conclude that you would do best to arrange a meeting with the latter. Charles Element will be pleased to outline for you a variety of mortgage as well as short-term loan plans.

All four major banks in town offer facilities for loans, so you may prefer to try them before or after meeting Mr Element. However, it certainly appears that our broker can secure more favourable conditions if you are interested principally in a short-term loan.

Please see our broker's details below:

Element Financial Services, Star Chambers, High Street, Worksop, Nottinghamshire.

Yours sincerely

Percy Hartshorn
Customer Liaison

Encs

51 Auskunft über Anleihen bzw. Hypotheken

14. Juli 199-

TV Becker GmbH
z. H. Herrn G. Bacher, Geschäftsleiter
Hölderlinstr. 59

87401 Kempten i. Allgäu

Sehr geehrter Herr Bacher,

seit dem Erhalt Ihres Briefes von 23. Juni haben wir uns über die von Ihnen erwähnten Finanzierungsmöglichkeiten hier erkundigt. Bitte entschuldigen Sie die daher verspätete Antwort. In der Anlage finden Sie drei Prospekte mit Information über Räumlichkeiten, die Sie interessieren dürften. Sie bedürfen keiner weiteren Erklärung[1] und wir erwarten Ihre Stellungnahme dazu.

Die Frage der Finanzierung ist vielleicht etwas drängender. Als Ergebnis unserer Erkundigungen bei den hiesigen Banken wie auch bei unserem eigenen Finanzmakler möchten wir Ihnen raten,[2] einen Termin mit letzterem zu vereinbaren. Herr Lederer wird Ihnen gerne einen Überblick über verschiedene Hypothekenarten und kurzfristige[3] Darlehen geben.

Da alle vier größeren Banken der Stadt Darlehen gewähren, wäre es vielleicht ratsam, sie vor oder nach Ihrer Besprechung mit Herrn Lederer zu konsultieren. Wenn Sie aber hauptsächlich nur an einem kurzfristigen Darlehen interessiert sind, ist unser Makler bestimmt besser in der Lage, Ihnen günstigere Bedingungen dafür zu vermitteln.

Hier die Adresse unseres Maklers:
Lederer Finanzen, Hauptplatz 26, 88003 Konstanz

Mit besten Grüßen

Paul Formann
Kundendienst

Anlage
Drei Prospekte

1 *Bedürfen* is used with the genitive. *Brauchen* and *benötigen* take the accusative.
2 *Raten* takes the dative. *Beraten* is used with the accusative.
3 *Kurzfristig*: 'short-term'. Medium-term: *mittelfristig*; long-term: *langfristig*.

52 Circulating local businesses with property services available

Our ref. CE/MB

To: Directors of all businesses in the
    Castilla-León region

Dear Colleague

I take the opportunity to write to you on behalf of myself and my partner in order to publicize as widely as possible the property services we can make available to businesses in the region.

Since establishing our company here in 1976 we have gradually expanded our range of activities and clients. Most recently we have opened a free advice centre in Puentenorte for any member of the public to obtain up-to-date information on the property market.

As regards the needs of business, we offer the following services:

- a weekly guide to premises for rent and sale
- a direct link to sources of finance
- rent-collection service
- legal and insurance consultancy
- assistance in securing mortgages
- technical support in planning space and furbishment
- computer database linked to the national property network

These and many more services are available from us, and all are on your doorstep. Don't hesitate – call us today, or come in person, when you can be sure of a warm welcome.

Yours sincerely

Carlos Estévez

52 Rundschreiben bezügl. Dienstleistungen einer Immobilienfirma

(Adresse)

Sehr geehrte Damen und Herren,

mein Geschäftspartner und ich möchten hiermit die Gelegenheit ergreifen, Sie auf unsere Dienstleistungen im Bereich Geschäftsimmobilien in Berlin und Umgebung aufmerksam zu machen.[1]

Seit der Gründung unserer Firma im Jahre 1976 haben wir unser Angebot und unseren Kundenkreis allmählich vergrößert. Mit der kürzlichen Eröffnung unseres Beratungszentrums in Berlin ist auch aktuelle Information über den Immobilienmarkt für jedermann kostenlos erhältlich.

Speziell für den unternehmerischen Bedarf bieten wir folgende Leistungen:

- ein wöchentliches Anzeigenblatt für Miet- und Kaufgelegenheiten
- direkte Verbindung zu Finanzquellen
- Mietkassierungsdienst
- Beratung in Rechts- und Versicherungsangelegenheiten
- Hilfe bei der Hypothekenerwerbung
- fachliche[2] Unterstützung bei Raumplanung und Möblierung
- Datenbank mit Anschluß an das überregionale Immobilien-Datennetz

Zu Ihrer weiteren Information stehen wir Ihnen gerne zur Verfügung. Wir würden uns über Ihren Anruf oder Besuch sehr freuen.[3]

Mit den besten Grüßen

Hermann Kunze

1 Alternative to *aufmerksam machen*: *Ihre Aufmerksamkeit auf . . . lenken.*
2 *Fachlich*: 'specialist'. Cf: *Fachleute*: 'experts', 'specialists'.
3 *Sich freuen über*: 'be pleased about'. *sich freuen auf*: 'to look forward to'.

53 Advertising maintenance services available for office equipment

30 January 199-

Your ref.
Our ref. TH/JY

To: Office Managers
     Motor Sales businesses
     in South London area

Dear Colleague

You may be aware from press advertising that our firm offers a new service to the motor trade, in particular to maintain equipment used in processing stores supplies. Most large dealerships with service and accessories departments have installed a fully integrated system that reduces drastically the need for large numbers of warehousemen.

The service charge is £350 per quarter, irrespective of visits made or problems solved; this figure also includes a component of insurance that covers both the dealership and ourselves against major breakdowns.

In recent months we have signed such service contracts with more than 40 dealerships whose names we are happy to supply if you are interested in checking our claims.

Thank you for your attention. Please do not hesitate to ring or fax us this week if the enclosed leaflet information is relevant to your needs.

Yours sincerely

Tom Henderson
Managing Director

Enc.

53 Rundschreiben bezügl. Wartung von Lagerhauskontrollsystemen

30. Januar 199-

(Adresse)

Sehr geehrte Damen und Herren,

unsere Firma ist Ihnen möglicherweise aus Pressewerbung bereits bekannt. Wir bieten einen neuartigen Service im Kfz-Handel[1] bezügl. der Wartung von elektronischen Lagerhauskontrollgeräten. Die meisten größeren Handelsunternehmen mit eigenen Kundendienst- und Zubehörabteilungen verfügen über ein einheitliches System, das die Zahl der notwendigen Lagerhausarbeiter wesentlich reduziert.

Die Service-Gebühr beträgt DM 805 pro Quartal unabhängig von Besuchen unserer Mitarbeiter oder Reparaturen. Dieser Betrag enthält auch einen Versicherungsbeitrag gegen Betriebsschäden auf beiden Seiten.

In den letzten Monaten kamen wir mit über 40 Händlern zum Abschluß eines Service-Vertrags. Zur Prüfung unserer Leistungen sind wir gern bereit, Ihnen eine Liste ihrer Namen zu übersenden.

Wir danken Ihnen für Ihr Interesse. Sollte die beiliegende Information auf Ihre Bedürfnisse zutreffen, würden wir uns freuen, von Ihnen telefonisch oder per Fax zu hören.

Mit freundlichen Grüßen

T. Hillinger
Geschäftsleiter

Anlage
Information

1 *Kfz*: abbreviation for *Kraftfahrzeug* ('vehicle').

54 Arranging a meeting for further discussions

28 August 199-

Our ref: TSS/EHK

Mr Angelo Ricasso
Cuscinetti SAS
Via Alessandro Manzoni, 32
20050 Triuggio (MI)
Italy

Dear Mr Ricasso

RE: THRUST BEARINGS

In 1989 we had discussions regarding the addition of our thrust bearings to the Dudley range for sale in your country.

We regret that due to many changes which have occurred in this company and in our parent company no progress was made with our arrangements, and we understand that it must have been disappointing for you not to have heard from us for such a long time.

We are now willing to try again, if you have not made other arrangements and we would like to arrange a meeting with you in Cologne at the Hardware Fair next March.

We look forward to hearing from you.

Yours sincerely

Thomas Stone
SALES DIRECTOR

54 Festsetzung eines weiteren Besprechungstermins

28. August 199-

Firma Steiner & Co
z.H. Herrn F. Steiner
Postfach 259

82400 München

Betrifft: Drucklager

Sehr geehrter Herr Steiner,

wir hatten im Jahre 1989 die Möglichkeit mit Ihnen besprochen, unsere Drucklager in die in Deutschland erhältliche Dudley Produktreihe aufzunehmen.

Es tut uns leid, daß aufgrund von betrieblichen Veränderungen bei uns sowie bei unserer Muttergesellschaft keinerlei Fortschritte in dieser Angelegenheit gemacht wurden, und wir verstehen Ihre Enttäuschung darüber, so lange nicht von uns gehört zu haben.

Falls Sie keine anderen Schritte unternommen haben, würden wir gerne noch einmal mit Ihnen über die Angelegenheit sprechen und möchten ein Treffen in Köln auf der Messe[1] für Eisenwaren im März vorschlagen.

Wir freuen uns, bald von Ihnen zu hören.

Mit besten Grüßen

T. Stone
Verkaufsleiter

1 *Auf der Messe*: 'at the trade fair'. Note the preposition.

111

55 Reservations

Enquiry about hotel accommodation (fax)

Hotel Lucullus
Amadeusplatz 27
Hannover
Germany

Dear Sirs

I am attending the trade fair in Hanover in May with two colleagues, and we require rooms for three nights. Please could you confirm availability and price of the following:

   three single rooms with bath/shower from 3 to 6 May.

Yours faithfully

Fred Garner

55 Reservierungen

Auskunft bezügl. Hotelunterkunft (Fax)

Hotel Lucullus
Amadeusplatz 27

D–30005 Hannover

Sehr geehrte Herren,

ich beabsichtige, die Hannoveraner Messe im Mai mit zwei meiner Kollegen zu besuchen und benötige daher Zimmer für drei Nächte. Könnten Sie bitte Tarif und Verfügbarkeit für drei Einzelzimmer mit Bad oder Dusche für die Zeit vom 3. bis 6. Mai bestätigen.

Mit freundlichen Grüßen

Fred Garner

56 Reservations

Confirmation of reservation (fax)

Ms G Cole
Ledington Parker plc
Moreton Avenue
Birmingham
B37 9KH

Dear Ms Cole

Room reservation 15–18 November

We confirm that we are able to offer the following accommodation:

Four single rooms with shower/WC @ £150 per night, inclusive of breakfast and service.

We should be grateful if you could confirm the booking in writing as soon as possible.

Yours sincerely

H Japer

56 Reservierungen

Bestätigung einer Buchung (Fax)

Föttinger & Co
z.H. Frau Gerda Kohl
Ringstr. 19

A 4600 Wels

Betr: Zimmerreservierung 15. – 18. November

Sehr geehrte Frau Kohl,

wir bestätigen, daß folgende Unterkunft verfügbar ist:

4 Einzelzimmer mit Dusche und WC zu DM 345 pro Nacht,[1] einschließlich Frühstück und Bedienung.

Wir wären Ihnen dankbar, wenn Sie Ihre Buchung so bald wie möglich schriftlich bestätigen könnten.

Mit besten Grüßen

H. Japer

1 Note the use of *zu* ('at 345 Marks').

57 Reservations

Change of arrival date

Ms J Hinton
Hotel Bonner
46 Southampton Way
London
SE39 8UH
England

Dear Madam

We have today received your confirmation of our booking of three single rooms from 18 to 23 March.

Unfortunately, we have had to change our plans, and shall not now arrive in London until the morning of 20 March. We would be grateful if you could change the reservation accordingly.

Yours faithfully

57 Reservierungsänderung

Hotel Bonner
z. H. Frau J. Hinton
46 Southampton Way

London
SE39 8UH
Großbritannien

Sehr geehrte Frau Hinton,

wir haben heute Ihre Bestätigung unserer Reservierung von drei Einbettzimmern
von 18. bis 23. März erhalten.

Leider mußten wir unsere Pläne ändern und werden daher erst am 20. März
vormittags in London ankommen. Bitte können Sie unsere Reservierung
dementsprechend abändern.

Mit freundlichen Grüßen

H. Klempner
Personalabteilung

58 Reservations

Request for confirmation of reservation

Ms J Petersen
45 Dorrington Terrace
Bradford
Yorkshire
England

Dear Ms Petersen

You made a telephone reservation one week ago for a single room for two nights (20–22 July). We indicated to you when you made the reservation that we would hold it for one week, but that we required written confirmation.

If you still require the room, could you please confirm within 24 hours, or we shall have to reserve the room for other clients.

Thank you for your co-operation.

Yours sincerely

58 Reservierungen

Ersuchen um Bestätigung

Frau J. Petersen
45 Dorrington Terrace

Bradford
Yorkshire
Großbritannien

Sehr geehrte Frau Petersen,

vor einer Woche reservierten Sie telefonisch ein Einbettzimmer für zwei Nächte (20. – 22. Juli). Dabei wiesen wir Sie darauf hin, daß wir das Zimmer eine Woche halten würden, aber eine schriftliche Bestätigung benötigten.

Bitte können Sie in den nächsten 24 Stunden bestätigen, daß Sie die Buchung noch wünschen, anderenfalls wird das Zimmer an andere Gäste vergeben.

Wir danken Ihnen für Ihr Verständnis.

Mit freundlichen Grüßen

J. Simpel

59 Insurance

Request for quotation for fleet car insurance

Hartson Insurance Services
24 Westbury Way
Sheffield
S12 9JF

Dear Sirs

We understand from colleagues that you specialize in insurance for company fleet cars. We have a large fleet of executive saloons, and are currently obtaining quotations for insurance cover.

If you are interested in giving us a quotation, could you please contact Ms Helen Bridges, our fleet manager, who will give you the appropriate details.

Yours faithfully

D J Spratt

59 Versicherung

Ersuchen um Angebot für Firmenwagenversicherung

Carstorp Versicherung
Westenbergstr. 24

14003 Potsdam

Sehr geehrte Damen und Herren,

von Geschäftsfreunden erfahren wir, daß Sie sich auf die Versicherung von Firmenwagen spezialisieren.[1] Wir verfügen über einen größeren Wagenpark bestehend aus Wagen der gehobenen Klasse, für die wir zur Zeit Versicherungsangebote einholen.

Wenn Sie uns ein Angebot machen wollen, wenden Sie sich bitte an Frau Helene Bruckner, Wagenparkverwaltung, um genauere Einzelheiten.

Mit freundlichen Grüßen

D. Späth

1 *Sich spezialisieren auf*: 'to specialize in'. Note the preposition. (But: *sich interessieren für*: 'to be interested in').

60 Insurance

Reminder of overdue premium

Mr R Collins
45 Delta Road
Stoke-on-Trent

Dear Mr Collins

Your vehicle, registration no H351 AWL is currently insured by us. We sent you
several days ago a reminder that the insurance renewal premium was due. As we
have still not received this from you, we have to inform you that unless we
receive payment within 72 hours, the insurance cover will lapse. Please send
payment directly to our office in Gower Street, London.

Yours sincerely

60 Versicherung

Mahnung bezügl. überfälliger Prämie

Herrn R. Koller
Dürerstr. 38

91000 Nürnberg

Sehr geehrter Herr Koller,

Ihr Fahrzeug, Kennzeichen NÜ 351 AW3, ist gegenwärtig bei uns versichert. Vor einiger Zeit schickten wir Ihnen eine Mahnung bezügl. der ausstehenden Zahlung Ihrer Erneuerungsprämie. Da wir diese bis jetzt noch nicht erhalten haben, müssen wir Ihnen mitteilen, daß Ihre Versicherung verfällt, wenn wir nicht binnen 72 Stunden Zahlung von Ihnen erhalten. Bitte überweisen Sie den Betrag direkt an unser Berliner Büro.[1]

Hochachtungsvoll

R. Mansion

1 *Überweisen an*: 'transfer to'. to transfer money to an account: *Geld auf ein Konto überweisen.*

61 Insurance

Submission of documents to support a claim

Darton Insurance Services
59 Tristan Road
Uttoxeter
Staffordshire

Dear Sirs

I submitted to you several days ago a claim form under the terms of my motor vehicle insurance (policy number CDF 9486756 UY 94766). Your head office has since requested from me the original policy document. I regret that this is no longer in my possession, and I enclose herewith a photocopy. I trust that this will meet your requirements.

Yours faithfully

A Lightowlers

Enc.

61 Versicherung

Vorlage von Dokumenten bei Versicherungsanspruch

MBS Versicherungsanstalt
Tristanstr. 41

4020 Linz

Sehr geehrte Herren,

vor einigen Tagen sandte ich Ihnen ein Formular zur Geltungmachung eines Anspruchs aufgrund meiner Kfz-Versicherung (Polizzennr. CDF 9486756 UY 94766). Von Ihrem Hauptbüro erhielt ich nun die Aufforderung, die Polizze im Original vorzulegen, was leider nicht möglich ist, da sich das Dokument nicht mehr in meinem Besitz befindet. Ich hoffe, Sie finden es akzeptabel, wenn ich daher eine Photokopie der Polizze beilege.

Mit freundlichen Grüßen

H. Beyer

Anlage
Photokopie

62 Insurance

Taking out third party vehicle insurance

Uxbridge Insurance
Grosvenor House
12b Weston Terrace
Bournemouth
Hants

Dear Sirs

After receiving your quotation, I confirm that I wish to take out Third Party car insurance, and enclose the appropriate fee in the form of a cheque.

I should be grateful if you could send me confirmation and the policy certificate as soon as possible.

Yours faithfully

Penny Simpkin

62 Versicherung

Abschluß einer Kfz-Haftpflichtversicherung[1]

Liebstock Versicherung
Am Hof 25

23000 Lübeck

Sehr geehrte Damen und Herren

Nach Erhalt Ihres Angebots bin ich bereit, eine Kfz-Haftpflichtversicherung abzuschließen und lege die entsprechende Gebühr in Form eines Schecks bei.

Für die möglichst baldige Übersendung der Polizze sowie einer Bestätigung wäre ich Ihnen dankbar.

Mit freundlichen Grüßen

G. Schubarth

1 *Kfz*: abbreviation for *Kraftfahrzeug* 'motor vehicle'.

63 Insurance

Refusal to meet claim

Ms D Leach
29 Janison Avenue
York

Dear Ms Leach

RE: CLAIM NO. JH 8576/HY

We acknowledge receipt of your claim form (reference JH 8576/HY) for water damage to your stock on the night of 27 March.

We regret, however, that our company is unable to meet your claim, as our policy (section 3, paragraph 5) specifically excludes this form of damage, particularly since the premises were unoccupied for a period of two weeks before the damage occurred.

Yours sincerely

P Hartwell

63 Versicherung

Ablehnung eines Anspruchs

Frau Dorte Becker
Rablstr. 37

44602 Dortmund

Sehr geehrte Frau Becker,

wir bestätigen den Empfang Ihres Antragsformulars (Zeichen JH 8576/HY)
bezügl.[1] des in der Nacht vom 27. Mai an Ihrem Warenlager entstandenen
Wasserschadens.

Leider sind wir nicht in der Lage, Ihrem Anspruch stattzugeben, da diese Art von
Schaden ausdrücklich als Versicherungsbegrenzung in Ihrer Polizze (Abschnitt 3,
Paragraph 5) aufscheint. Noch dazu wurden die Geschäftsräume vor der
Entstehung des Schadens zwei Wochen lang nicht benützt.

Mit freundlichen Grüßen

P. Stark

1 *Bezügl.*: abbreviation of *bezüglich*. Takes the genitive.

64 Considering legal action

24 May 199-

Cabinet Rossignol
4 rue des Glaïeuls
75009 Paris
France

For the attention of Maître Patelin

Dear Maître Patelin

Your name was given to us by Robert Mackenzie of Canine Crunch Ltd for whom you acted last year.

We have a complaint against the newspaper *La Gazette du Samedi* who have, in our opinion, seriously defamed us in the enclosed article dealing with the closure of our plant at Roissy-en-France.

We would wish to take legal action against the said journal but first would like to have your professional advice on the strength of our case. Could you also let us know how long such a case might run and the likely scale of our legal costs.

Yours sincerely

Lionel E Bone
Managing Director

Enc.

64 Erwägung des Rechtsweges

Herrn
Dr. Franz Billig
Rechtsanwalt
Heinrich-Heine-Str. 72

D–53000 Bonn

Sehr geehrter Herr Dr. Billig,

wir wenden uns an Sie auf Vorschlag von Herrn Robert Mackenzie von der Firma Canine Crunch Ltd, für die Sie im letzten Jahr als Rechtsvertreter fungierten.

Wir erheben Beschwerde gegen die Zeitung 'Samstagsblatt', die sich unserer Meinung nach in dem beiliegenden Artikel über die Stillegung unserer Fabrik in Mönchengladbach einer schweren Defamierung unserer Firma schuldig macht.

Wir sind bereit, gegen die besagte Zeitung zu prozessieren, möchten aber vorerst Ihren fachmännischen[1] Rat mit Bezug auf die Stichhaltigkeit unseres Falles einholen. Könnten Sie uns auch gleichzeitig über die erwartete Prozeßdauer und die voraussichtlichen Gerichtskosten unterrichten.

MIt besten Grüßen

Lionel E. Bone
Geschäftsleiter

Anlage

Artikel

---

1 *Fachmännisch*: 'expert'. Note also: *Fachmann* (pl. *Fachleute*); 'expert'. *Fachgebiet*: 'specialist area', 'specialism'.

65 Requesting information on setting up a plant abroad

23 May 199-

Office Notarial
84 rue du Grand Pineau
85000 Olonnes sur Mer
France

Dear Sirs

Our company is proposing to set up a dairy produce processing plant in western France and we would like you to find us a suitable site.

We need either freehold or leasehold premises of 2,000 square metres on a plot with easy access for large vehicles.

Can you help us in finding the site and act for us in its acquisition? This is our first venture into France so we would appreciate all additional information about property purchase or leasing.

Yours faithfully

Arthur Sturrock
Managing Director

65 Erkundigung über Gründung einer Produktionsanlage im Ausland

23. Mai 199-

Notariatskanzlei Dr. S. Grasskamp
Fontaneweg 37

D–17236 Greifswald

Sehr geehrte Damen und Herren,

unser Unternehmen beabsichtigt, in Ostdeutschland eine Anlage zur Konservierung von Molkereiprodukten einzurichten,[1] und wir möchten Sie ersuchen, uns ein geeignetes Gelände zu finden.

Wir benötigen eine gewerbliche Nutzfläche von etwa 2000m², entweder zum Verkauf oder zur Pacht, auf einem für große Fahrzeuge leicht zugänglichen Grundstück.

Wir wären Ihnen dankbar für Ihre Hilfe bei der Suche und beim Erwerb einer Anlage. Da dies unser erstes Geschäftsprojekt in Deutschland ist, wäre uns jede zusätzliche Information über Kauf oder Pacht von Liegenschaften äußerst willkommen.

Mit freundlichen Grüßen

Arthur Sturrock
Geschäftsführer

1 *Eine Anlage einrichten*: set up, establish a plant; *gründen* would also be possible.

66 Complaint about delay in administering an account

18 September 199-

Société Bancaire Générale
4 boulevard Leclerc
76200 Dieppe
France

For the attention of the Manager

Dear Sir

RE: ACCOUNT NO. 654231

We have received the July statement of our above account no. 654231 and are surprised that the balance shown is so low.

We have been assured by two of our major customers, Alligand SA and Berthaud Etains, that they settled large outstanding invoices by bank transfer to that account four weeks and five weeks ago respectively.

Will you please check our account very carefully and let us know the exact balance by fax. If as we think, work is being processed by you in a dilatory fashion, please could you let us know the reason for this.

Yours sincerely

Eric Smith
Finance Director

66 Beschwerde über Kontenverwaltung

18. September 199-

An die Direktion
der Allgemeinen Wirtschaftsbank
Stolzingplatz 78

D–90000 Nürnberg

Sehr geehrte Damen und Herren,

wir erhielten soeben den Juli-Auszug unseres Kontos Nr. 654231 und sind
erstaunt über den niedrigen Kontostand.

Zwei wichtige Kunden, Wanninger AG und Kleinwerth & Sohn, haben uns
versichert,[1] daß sie vor vier bzw. fünf Wochen größere Summen als Begleichung
ausstehender Rechnungen auf unser Konto überwiesen haben.

Könnten Sie unser Konto noch einmal überprüfen und uns den genauen Stand
per Fax übermitteln oder uns eine Erklärung für die unserer Ansicht nach
ungebührliche Verzögerung in Ihrer Verwaltung geben.

Mit besten Grüßen

Eric Smith
Finanzleiter

1 *Haben uns versichert*: the *uns* is in the dative – 'they assured us.' Note: *Versichern* +
accusative: 'to insure'.

67 Complaint about mail delivery

19 November 199-

The Central Post Office
Place Centrale
53000 Laval
France

Dear Sirs

As a result of enquiries we have made in England it appears that delays we have experienced in the delivery of our mail to our subsidiary in Cossé le Vivien are being caused at the Laval sorting office.

Since our business is being seriously inconvenienced by postal delays we would be most grateful if you could look into the matter.

It should not take 10 days for orders and invoices to get from us to our colleagues in Cossé. Enclosed is a sample mailing where you can see the dates clearly marked.

Yours faithfully

Jeremy P Johnson
Director

Enc.

67 Beschwerde über Postzustellung

19. November 199-

Zentralpostamt
Fadingerstr. 38

D 80001 München

Sehr geehrte Damen und Herren,

unseren Erkundigungen in England zufolge scheint es, daß die Verzögerung in
der Postzustellung an unsere Niederlassung in Holzkirchen von der Sortierstelle
in München verursacht wird.

Da unsere Geschäfte durch die langsame Postzustellung ernstlich beeinträchtigt
werden, möchten wir Sie bitten, die Angelegenheit zu untersuchen.

Es sollte nicht vorkommen, daß Aufträge und Rechnungen 10 Tage von uns nach
Holzkirchen unterwegs sind, wie Sie dem Beispiel des beiliegenden Briefes mit
deutlich markierten Daten entnehmen können.[1]

Mit freundlichen Grüßen

Jeremy P. Johnson
Direktor

Anlage

Brief

1 *Entnehmen* does not require a preposition, simply the dative. *Sie entnehmen meinem
   Brief...*: 'you see from my letter' ...

68 Complaint about wrong consignment of goods

1 September 199-

Dessous Dessus
14 rue Legrand
80000 Amiens
France

<u>For the attention of Mr A Malraux</u>

Dear Mr Malraux

<u>RE: INVOICE NO. 13322/08/92</u>

We regret to inform you that the garments you sent us in your consignment of 25 August were not what we had ordered.

If you refer to our order (copy enclosed) and to your invoice, you will see that the briefs, slips and bras are mostly the wrong sizes, colours and materials.

We are at a loss to explain this departure from your normally reliable service. Will you please contact us immediately so that we can put matters right?

Yours sincerely

Fred Smith
Manager

Enc.

68 Beschwerde über falsche Lieferung

1. September 199-

Palmer Dessous
Wedekindstr. 39

D–76000 Karlsruhe

Zu Händen von Herrn A. Brecht

Sehr geehrter Herr Brecht,

wir müssen Ihnen leider mitteilen, daß Ihre Lieferung vom 25. August nicht unserem Auftrag entspricht.

Wie Sie aus der beiliegenden Kopie unseres Auftrags und aus Ihrer Rechnung ersehen können, handelt es sich bei den Höschen, Unterkleidern und Büstenhaltern zumeist um die falschen Größen, Farben und das falsche Material.

Wir können uns nicht erklären, warum Ihr normalerweise verläßlicher Geschäftsbetrieb diesmal nicht funktionierte und möchten Sie ersuchen, die Angelegenheit so bald wie möglich richtig zu stellen.

Mit freundlichen Grüßen

Fred Smith
Geschäftsführer

Anlage
Auftrag

69 Complaint about damage to goods

3 April 199-

Transports Transmanche SA
Quai des Brumes
14000 Caen
France

For the attention of Mr Gérard Dispendieux

Dear Monsieur Dispendieux

We have received a complaint from John Ferguson of Amex Insurance concerning their removal to Beauvais. You will remember that we subcontracted this removal to your company.

Mr Ferguson claims that several of the items of furniture and office equipment were damaged on arrival at the premises in Beauvais.

Although he immediately complained to your deliverymen, he has still not heard from your company. In the interests of our future business relations I would be grateful if you could clarify this situation.

Yours sincerely

Gerald Wagstaffe
French Area Manager

69 Beschwerde über Warenschäden

3. April 199-

Spedition Jensen GmbH
Friesendeichstr. 48

D 28207 Bremerhaven

Zu Händen von Herrn W. Wenders

Sehr geehrter Herr Wenders,

wir erhielten eine Beschwerde von Herrn John Ferguson, Firma Amex
Versicherung, bezüglich ihrer Übersiedlung nach Magdeburg. Wie Sie wissen,
hatten wir Ihre Firma für diese Unternehmung unter Vertrag genommen.

Herr Ferguson behauptet, daß etliche[1] Möbelstücke und Bürogeräte bei der
Ankunft in Magdeburg beschädigt waren.

Obwohl er sich sofort beim Transportpersonal beschwert hatte, hat er bis jetzt
noch keine weitere Nachricht von Ihrer Firma. Wir möchten Sie daher ersuchen,
die Angelegenheit im Interesse unserer zukünftigen Geschäftsbeziehungen zu
klären.

Mir freundlichen Grüßen

Gerald Wagstaffe
Gebietsleiter für Deutschland

1 *Etliche*: 'quite a few', 'many'. This word is very formal and not particularly common. It
would be little used in spoken German.

70 Informing customers that a company has been taken over

24 July 199-

Produits Chimiques SA
89 rue Jules Barni
80330 Longueau
France

Dear Sirs

Thank you for your order dated 17 July. We have to inform you, however, that our company has recently been taken over by a larger concern, International Chemicals Inc.

As a result of this, we no longer produce the polymers that you request at this site. We have however passed on your order to our parent company and are confident that you will be contacted soon.

In the interests of our future business relations we enclose the latest catalogue of our total range of products, indicating which subsidiary manufactures which product.

Yours faithfully

Frederick Herriot
Plant Director

Enc.

70 Mitteilung über Firmenübernahme

24. Juli 199-

Neckarchemie AG
Postfach 375

68000 Mannheim

Sehr geehrte Herren,

wir danken Ihnen für Ihren Auftrag vom 17.07. und möchten Ihnen gleichzeitig die Übernahme unseres Betriebs durch den Großkonzern International Chemicals Inc. bekanntgeben.

Außerdem müssen wir Ihnen mitteilen, daß wir die von Ihnen benötigten Polymere nicht mehr herstellen. Wir haben jedoch Ihre Bestellung an unsere Mutterfirma[1] weitergeleitet und sind sicher, daß Sie demnächst benachrichtigt werden. ·

Im Interesse unserer zukünftigen Geschäftsbeziehungen legen wir den neuesten Katalog unserer gesamten Produktpalette bei mit dem Hinweis auf die betreffenden Herstellerfirmen unserer Gruppe.[2]

Mit besten Grüßen

Frederick Herriot
Werksleiter

Anlage
Katalog

1 *Mutterfirma*: 'parent company'. Note also *Tochtergesellschaft*: 'subsidiary'.
2 Note the word order here. *Bei* would be expected to be at the end of the sentence. It is placed here because of the long phrase which follows.

71 Informing customers of change of name and address

EUROPEAN COMMERCIAL INSURANCE Ltd
47 Broad Walk
Preston
Lancashire United Kingdom

(Formerly PRESTON INSURERS Inkerman Street, Preston)

1 June 199-

The Export Manager
Nouveaux Textiles
342 chaussée Baron
59100 Roubaix
France

Dear Sir

RE: CHANGE OF COMPANY NAME AND ADDRESS

We are writing to all our valued customers to inform them that we have changed both our registered name and our address.

We are still located in Preston and operating as commercial insurers as before. However, we have acquired new partners who have invested fresh capital in the business.

It is our intention to increase our European business, hence the new name. Enclosed is our brochure setting out our range of services and tariffs. Do not hesitate to contact us if you have any queries about these changes.

Yours faithfully

Nancy Wilton
Customer Liaison Manager

Enc.

71 Kundenavis – Namens- und Adressenänderung

European Commercial Insurance Ltd
47 Broad Walk
Preston
Lancashire
United Kingdom

(Vormals Preston Insurers, Inkerman Street, Preston)

1. Juni 199-

Epple Maschinenbau AG
Exportabteilung
Postfach 486

D–61007 Frankfurt

Sehr geehrte Damen und Herren,

wir möchten hiermit unsere werten Kunden davon in Kenntnis setzen, daß wir sowohl unseren eingetragenen Namen als auch unsere Adresse geändert haben.

Unsere Firma befindet sich nach wie vor in Preston und fungiert weiterhin als gewerbliche Versicherungsanstalt. Durch die Aufnahme neuer Geschäftspartner floß frisches Investitionskapital in unser Unternehmen.

Unsere Namensänderung rührt von der Absicht, unseren europäischen Geschäftsbereich zu erweitern. In der Anlage[1] finden Sie eine Broschüre mit unseren Dienstleistungen und Tarifen. Sollten Sie irgendwelche Fragen über diese Veränderungen haben, bitte zögern Sie nicht, sich an uns zu wenden.

Mit besten Grüßen

Nancy Wilson
Kundendienstleitung

<u>Anlage</u>
Broschüre

---

1 *In der Anlage*: enclosed. Also possible would be: *als Anlage; wir legen . . . bei.*

72 Informing customers of increased prices

12 November 199-

Epicerie Fine
9 rue Dutour
72100 Le Mans
France

Dear Monsieur Olivier

In reply to your letter of the 5th I am sending you a new price list.

You will note that all of our prices have increased by some 6.3 per cent. This was unfortunately made necessary by our continuing inflation as well as the British Chancellor's recent decision to increase the general rate of VAT to 17.5 per cent.

I hope, however, that the quality of our produce will continue to engage your loyalty. It is also the case that the pound sterling has reduced in value.

Yours sincerely

Michael McDermott
Marketing Manager

Enc.

72 Kundenavis – Preiserhöhung

12. November 199-

Feinkost Derflinger
Ringstr. 79

D 66000 Saarbrücken

Sehr geehrter Herr Derflinger,

in Antwort auf Ihren Brief vom 5. d. M. sende ich Ihnen eine neue Preisliste.

Sie werden ersehen, daß alle unsere Preise um[1] etwa 6,3% gestiegen sind. Dies ist leider auf die anhaltende Inflation zurückzuführen und auch auf die jüngste Entscheidung des britischen Schatzkanzlers, die Mehrwertsteuer auf 17,5% zu erhöhen.

Ich hoffe aber, daß Sie uns aufgrund der Güte unserer Erzeugnisse Ihre Kundentreue bewahren werden (ungeachtet der Tatsache, daß auch nun das Pfund Sterling an Wert verloren hat).

Mit besten Grüßen

Michael McDermott
Marketingleiter

Anlage
Preisliste

---

1 *Um*: 'by', is used with all verbs of increasing or decreasing. Such verbs also add *auf*: 'to' (as with *erhöhen auf* below).

73 Requesting information about opening a business account

23 October 199-

The Manager
Crédit Mercantile
89 rue Béranger
69631 VÉNISSIEUX
France

Dear Sir

We are proposing to open an office and refrigerated storage facility at Vénissieux in the new year and would appreciate some information about opening a bank account at your branch.

Initially we would be transferring funds to finance the setting up of our new business premises. Thereafter we would expect to use the account to receive payments from French customers and to pay local suppliers etc.

We would be most grateful if you could inform us of all the formalities that we need to observe, both public and particular, to Crédit Mercantile. Could you also inform us of your charges on business accounts?

Yours faithfully

Eric Wise
Commercial Manager

73 Erkundigung über Eröffnung eines Geschäftskontos

23. Oktober 199-

An die Direktion
Gewerbebank
Hohenzollernplatz 58

D 07370 Neubrandenburg

Sehr geehrte Herren,

wir beabsichtigen, im kommenden Jahre eine Geschäftsstelle sowie
Kühlräume in Neubrandenburg zu eröffnen und möchten gerne Auskunft über
die Eröffnung eines Kontos bei Ihrer Bank.

Anfänglich würden wir Beträge zur Einrichtung unserer Geschäftsräume
überweisen, später würden wir das Konto zur Abrechnung mit unseren
deutschen Kunden und Lieferanten verwenden.

Wir wären Ihnen dankbar, wenn Sie uns über alle notwendigen Formalitäten in
der Bank und im allgemeinen Auskunft geben könnten. Könnten Sie uns auch
gleichzeitig Ihre Gebühren bei Geschäftskonten mitteilen.

Mit freundlichen Grüßen

Eric Wise
Geschäftsleiter

74 Requesting information about opening a personal bank account

4 November 199-

The Manager
Banque Nationale
146 boulevard Haussmann
75016 Paris
France

Dear Sir

My British employers are posting me to their French subsidiary and I will therefore be moving to Paris with my family and expect to be resident in France for two years.

Would you please let me have details about opening a personal current account at your bank. My salary would be paid into the account and I would wish to draw money from it and to pay bills by cheque etc. I may also wish to transfer money to a bank account in England.

I would be grateful for any documentation you can send me.

Yours faithfully

Stuart Smith

74 Erkundigung über Eröffnung eines Privatkontos

4. November 199-

Bank für Hessen
Kontenabteilung
Krönungsallee 37

D–60000 Frankfurt

Sehr geehrte Damen und Herren,

aufgrund meiner Versetzung von England in unsere deutsche Filiale werde ich mit meiner Familie nach Frankfurt übersiedeln und dort voraussichtlich zwei Jahre wohnhaft sein.

Könnten Sie mir bitte Information über die Eröffnung eines Privatgirokontos bei Ihrer Bank zukommen lassen. Das Konto sollte die Funktion eines Gehalts-, Zahlungs- und Scheckkontos haben. Möglicherweise würde es auch zur Geldüberweisung auf ein englisches Konto benützt werden.

Ich wäre Ihnen dankbar für die Übersendung von Informationsmaterial in dieser Angelegenheit.

Mit freundlichen Grüßen

Stuart Smith

75 Letter re overdrawn account

9 March 199-

J H Jameson
47 Narrow Bank
Lichfield
Staffordshire

Dear Mr Jameson

We regret to inform you that your account, number 62467840, is overdrawn by £21.09.

We would appreciate your rectifying this situation as soon as possible since you have no overdraft arrangement with us.

Yours sincerely

F E Jones
Manager

75 Kontoüberziehung

9. März 199-

Herrn
Heinrich Höllerer
Gablerstr. 34

52061 Bochum

Sehr geehrter Herr Höllerer,

wir müssen Ihnen leider mitteilen, daß Ihr Konto, Nr. 62647840, um DM 48,83 überzogen ist.

Da Sie über keinen Dispositionskredit bei uns verfügen, müssen wir Sie ersuchen, diese Angelegenheit ehestens zu bereinigen.

Mit besten Grüßen

F. Jocher
Direktor

76 Bank's letter to customer

2 May 199-

Mr Bernard J Mann
4 Beauchamp Mews
London
England

Dear Mr Mann

We are writing to inform you that we have today received a cheque payable to you for the sum of $124,035.00 and sent by J et P Barraud Notaires, 307 rue du Château, Luxembourg.

Can you please confirm as soon as possible that you were expecting this deposit and let us know your instructions concerning it?

Enclosed is a photocopy of this cheque and its accompanying letter.

Yours sincerely

Amélie Dupont
Head Cashier

Encs

76 Bankschreiben an Kunden

2. Mai 199-

Mr. Bernhard J. Mann
4 Beauchamp Mews

London
Großbritiannien

Sehr geehrter Herr Mann,

wir teilen Ihnen mit, daß wir heute einen auf Ihren Namen ausgestellten Scheck[1] über[2] DM 190 035,- von der Notariatskanzlei P. Lützeler, 307 rue du Château, Luxemburg, erhalten haben.

Könnten Sie so bald wie möglich bestätigen, daß Sie diese Einlage erwarten und uns Ihre diesbezüglichen Anweisungen übermitteln.

In der Anlage finden sie eine Photokopie des Schecks und des Begleitschreibens.

Mit freundlichen Grüßen

Amanda Bruckner
Hauptkassier

<u>Anlage</u>
Zwei Photokopien

1 *Einen Scheck ausstellen*: 'to make out a cheque'. 'Crossed cheque': *Verrechnungsscheck*.
2 *Ein Scheck über*: 'a cheque for' (the amount of) . . .

77 General query about banking

Monsieur J. Delor
Président-Directeur Général
Mouton-Poulenc
7 rue du Trocadéro
Paris 3 Cedex
France

Dear Sir

In response to your general query about banking in England there are two main types of bank, merchant banks and commercial banks. The former are very numerous and deal with companies generally. The latter are mainly the four big groups, Lloyds, National Westminster, Barclays and Midland.

The enclosed leaflet will give you further details, including information about banking in Scotland. The Ombudsman's office is mainly concerned with complaints about banks.

You should note that The Post Office in England also has some banking and money transfer facilities.

Yours faithfully

C D Prettyman
For the Ombudsman

Enc.

77 Allgemeine Bankinformation

Herrn Generaldirektor
Dr. Erich Panther
EXI Werke
Händelstr. 24

D–04862 Halle

Sehr geehrter Herr Generaldirektor,

wir beantworten[1] gerne Ihre Anfrage bezügl. des englischen Bankwesens. Generell gibt es zwei Arten von Banken, Handelsbanken und allgemeine Kreditinstitute. Erstere sind zahlreich und sind vornehmlich für Geschäftsunternehmen tätig; zur letzteren gehören hauptsächlich die vier Großbanken Lloyds, National Westminster, Barclays und Midland.

Die beiliegende Broschüre gibt Ihnen weitere Einzelheiten sowie Auskunft über das Bankwesen in Schottland. Unser Amt ist vor allem für Bankbeschwerden zuständig.

Außerdem möchten wir Sie darauf hinweisen, daß auch die Post gewisse Geldüberweisungs- und andere Bankgeschäfte übernimmt.

Mit besten Grüßen

C.D.Prettyman
i.A. Ombudsman

Anlage
Broschüre

1 'To answer': *beantworten* or *antworten auf.*

78 Enquiry about post office banking facilities

2 February 199-

La Poste Centrale
Place Général De Gaulle
16000 Angoulême
France

Dear Sirs

I am intending to open a second business in Angoulême and would like to enquire what services you offer to small businesses.

I have in mind giro banking; can you tell me how your post office bank accounts work? Secondly, is it to you that I should apply to have a telephone? Thirdly, do you have special rates for business mail?

I would be most grateful for any information you can send me.

Yours faithfully

Mostyn Evans
Proprietor

78 Anfrage bezügl. Bankdienste der Post

2. Februar 199-

An das Hauptpostamt
Westfalenplatz 48

D 48000 Münster

Sehr geehrte Damen und Herren,

wir beabsichtigen, eine Niederlassung in Münster zu eröffnen und möchten uns über Ihr Dienstleistungsangebot für Kleinunternehmer erkundigen.

Könnten Sie uns bitte genauere Einzelheiten bezügl. eines Postscheckkontos geben? Sollen wir das Ansuchen um einen Telefonanschluß an Ihre Adresse richten? Und schließlich möchten wir wissen, ob es Sondergebühren für geschäftlichen Briefverkehr gibt.

Für Ihre diesbezüglichen Informationen wären wir Ihnen äußerst dankbar.

Mit freundlichen Grüßen

Mostyn Evans
Inhaber

79 Enquiry about opening a post office account

8 March 199-

Bureau Central
Postes et Télécommunications
Paris
France

Dear Sirs

I do not know exactly who to write to and hope that this letter will reach the right service.

I wish to obtain information about opening a Post Office account in France, to facilitate financial transactions with my French customers and suppliers.

Will you please inform me of your formalities and send me the necessary forms?

Yours faithfully

Eric Clifford
Managing Director

79 Erkundigung bezügl. Postscheckkonto

8. März 199-

An das
Bundeszentralamt für Post- und Telekommunikation

D–10000 Berlin

Sehr geehrte Damen und Herren,

mangels einer Kontaktadresse wende ich mich an Sie mit der Bitte, diesen Brief nötigenfalls[1] an die richtige Stelle weiterzuleiten.

Ich ersuche um Auskunft über die Eröffnung eines Postscheckkontos in Deutschland zur Abrechnung mit meinen deutschen Kunden und Lieferanten.

Bitte könnten Sie mir über etwaige Formalitäten Bescheid geben und mir die erforderlichen Formulare zukommen lassen.[2]

Mit besten Grüßen

Eric Clifford
Betriebsleiter

1 Alternative to *nötigenfalls*: *wenn nötig*.
2 *Zukommen lassen* is rather formal. *Schicken* or *senden* would be just as acceptable.

80 Opening poste restante

18 April 199-

La Poste Centrale
Place Bellecour
69001 Lyon
France

Gentlemen

We are in the process of moving our French subsidiary from Villeurbanne to Saint Priest; the move should be completed some time in the next month.

Could we ask you on receipt of this letter, and until further notice, to retain all mail addressed to us poste restante at your central office?

Please inform us if there are any other formalities to observe. Enclosed is an addressed envelope and international reply coupon for your reply.

Thank you in advance.

Arthur T Goldberg
On behalf of Software Supplies Inc.

Enc.

80 Eröffnung einer Aufbewahrungsstelle für postlagernde Sendungen

An das Hauptpostamt
Innufer 40

D–94000 Passau

Sehr geehrte Damen und Herren,

wir sind im Begriff, unsere deutsche Tochterfirma von Dingolfing nach Plattling zu verlegen. In etwa einem Monat dürfte die Übersiedlung abgeschlossen sein.

Wir möchten Sie ersuchen, nach Erhalt dieses Briefes alle an uns adressierten Postsendungen bis auf weiteres in Ihrer Zentrale postlagernd aufzubewahren.

Bitte teilen Sie uns mit, ob andere Formalitäten zu erledigen sind. Für Ihre Antwort liegt ein adressierter Umschlag und ein internationaler Antwortschein bei.

Besten Dank im voraus.

i.A. Arthur T. Goldberg

Anlage
Adressierter Umschlag
Internationaler Antwortschein